Progressive Steps in Architectural Drawing

By
· Geo· W· Seaman · ▼ Architect ·
· Instructor· In· Architecture ▼ School· of· Industrial · Arts ·
Trenton · ▼ N·J

▼ A· Step-by-step· Method· for· Student-Draughtsmen · ▼▼
Together with· Details· of· Construction· & Design·

Copyright © 2013 Read Books Ltd.
This book is copyright and may not be
reproduced or copied in any way without
the express permission of the publisher in writing

British Library Cataloguing-in-Publication Data
A catalogue record for this book is available from the
British Library

Technical Drawing and Drafting

Technical drawing, also known as 'drafting' or 'draughting', is the act and discipline of composing plans that visually communicate how something functions or is to be constructed.

It is essential for communicating ideas in industry, architecture and engineering. The need for precise communication in the preparation of a functional document distinguishes technical drawing from the expressive drawing of the visual arts. Whereas artistic drawings are subjectively interpreted, with multiply determined meanings, technical drawings generally have only one intended meaning. To make the drawings easier to understand, practitioners use familiar symbols, perspectives, units of measurement, notation systems, visual styles, and page layout. Together, such conventions constitute a visual language, and help to ensure that the drawing is unambiguous and relatively easy to understand.

There are many methods of constructing a technical drawing, and most simple among them is a sketch. A sketch is a quickly executed, freehand drawing that is not intended as a finished work. In general, sketching is a quick way to record an idea for later use, and architects sketches in particular (in a very similar manner to fine artists) serve as a way to try out different ideas and establish a composition before undertaking more finished work. Architects drawings can also be used to convince clients of the merits of a design, to enable a building constructer to use them, and as a record of completed work. In a similar manner to engineering (and all other technical drawings), there is a set of conventions (i.e particular views, measurements, scales, and cross-referencing) that are utilised.

As opposed to free-sketching, technical drawings usually utilise various manuals and instruments. The basic drafting procedure is to place a piece of paper (or other material) on a smooth surface with right-angle corners and straight sides – typically a drawing board. A sliding straightedge known as a 'T-square' is then placed on one of the sides, allowing it to be slid across the side of the table, and over the surface of the paper. Parallel lines can be drawn simply by moving the T-square and running a pencil along the edge, as well as holding devices such as set squares or triangles. Other tools can be used to draw curves and circles, and primary among these are the compasses, used for drawing simple arcs and circles. Drafting templates are also utilised in cases where the drafter has to create recurring objects in a drawing – a massive time-saving development.

This basic drafting system requires an accurate table and constant attention to the positioning of the tools. A common error is to allow the triangles to push the top of the T-square down slightly, thereby throwing off all the angles. Even tasks as simple as drawing two angled lines meeting at a point require a number of moves of the T-square and triangles, and in general drafting this can be a time consuming process. In addition to the mastery of the mechanics of drawing lines, arcs, circles (and text) onto a piece of paper – the drafting effort requires a thorough understanding of geometry, trigonometry and spatial comprehension. In all cases, it demands precision and accuracy, and attention to detail.

Conventionally, drawings were made in ink on paper or a similar material, and any copies required had to be laboriously made by hand. The twentieth century saw a shift to drawing on tracing paper, so that mechanical copies could be run off efficiently. This was a substantial development in the drafting process – only eclipsed in the twenty-first century with 'computer-aided-drawing' systems (CAD). Although classical draftsmen and women are still in high demand, the mechanics of the drafting task have largely been automated and accelerated through the use of such systems. The development of the computer had a major impact on the methods used to design and create technical drawings, making manual drawing almost obsolete, and opening up new possibilities of form using organic shapes and complex geometry.

Today, there are two types of computer-aided design systems used for the production of technical drawings; two dimensions ('2D') and three dimensions ('3D'). 2D CAD systems such as AutoCAD or MicroStation have largely replaced the paper drawing discipline. Lines, circles, arcs and curves are all created within the software. It is down to the technical drawing skill of the user to produce the drawing – though this method does allow for the making of numerous revisions, and modifications of original designs. 3D CAD systems such as Autodesk Inventor or SolidWorks first produce the geometry of the part, and the technical drawing comes from user defined views of the part. This means there is little scope for error once the parameters have been set.

Buildings, Aircraft, ships and cars are now all modelled, assembled and checked in 3D before technical drawings are released for manufacture.

Technical drawing is a skill that is essential for so many industries and endeavours, allowing complex ideas and designs to become reality. It is hoped that the current reader enjoys this book on the subject.

INTRODUCTION

In presenting this work it has been the purpose of the writer to follow a definite system of draughtsmanship, and to explain the various steps taken so that they will act as a guide to the young student-draughtsman. As a rule the student knows how the finished product should appear, but seldom has he any definite idea of how best to obtain this result. He will find himself drawing line after line without their having any meaning to him; in some cases using another drawing as an example, counting the lines of the cornice, belt course or other details and laying great stress on the *number* of lines used, but knowing little of their meaning or effect.

Very often in the classroom the student will be found working earnestly over unimportant features of the plan or elevation before he has worked out broadly the whole drawing. This often brings his work to an abrupt stop, and he has no idea of how to proceed with his drawing in a practical manner. Had the student blocked out the plans and elevations in their entirety, he would have at once obtained a grasp of the problem which would have enabled him to carry out his work to a successful completion.

The experienced draughtsman must not judge the beginner too severely for any mistakes which he may make. The student is practically learning a new language, and therefore he must acquire the proper pronunciation and meaning of the "words", step by step, before he can readily "talk" (or draw) with his pencil in a creditable manner.

It is, therefore, in the hope of assisting the student-draughtsman to acquire a definite method in the laying out of his work that the following is respectfully submitted.

Trenton, New Jersey,
February, 1919.

GEO. W. SEAMAN.

CONTENTS

	PAGE
INTRODUCTION	3
PROFESSIONAL PRACTICE	7
PRACTICAL HINTS ON DRAWING	10
Plans	10
Room Sizes	10
Walls	11
Interior Details	11
Fixtures	12
Elevations	12
Exterior Details	12
PROGRESSIVE STEPS IN THE DEVELOPMENT OF PLANS	14
PROGRESSIVE STEPS IN THE DEVELOPMENT OF ELEVATIONS	24
VARIATIONS IN PLANS AND ELEVATIONS	32
PROGRESSIVE STEPS IN THE DRAWING OF CORNICES ON ONE-QUARTER INCH SCALE ELEVATIONS	38
PROGRESSIVE STEPS IN THE DRAWING OF PORCH CORNICES AND COLUMNS AT ONE-QUARTER INCH SCALE	40
PROGRESSIVE STEPS IN DRAWING DETAILS OF DOUBLE-HUNG WINDOW FRAMES AT SCALE OR FULL SIZE	43
PROGRESSIVE STEPS IN THE DRAWING OF THREE-QUARTER AND FULL SIZE DETAILS	46
MOULDINGS AND PROFILES	48

PROFESSIONAL PRACTICE

The usual freehand sketch-plans and elevations, drawn by the architect on the back of an envelope or bit of scrap paper, either during or just following his consultation with the future client, are reproduced in a typical manner on Plate 1. This sketch may be the result of a dozen or more attempts of the architect to interpret his client's requirements, or he may have been successful in the first attempt. Plates 27, 28, 29 and 30 should also be studied for further information, reference, and practice in making sketch-plans.

The size of rooms, their position in the plan, style and size of house, its location and the materials to be used will have all been thoroughly discussed. The method of heating and lighting, and also the quality and style of the plumbing fixtures will have been settled upon, and the important question of cost taken up.

The architect then gives these rough sketches to one of his draughtsmen with instructions to "work it up". Thickness and material for the outside walls are determined, and also any special features of design either in plan or elevation, which might well be worked into the drawings. Sometimes a start is made at once on $\frac{1}{4}$" scale working drawings, but more often the plans and elevations are worked up at $\frac{1}{8}$" scale, and submitted to the client for his approval before starting the final drawings. On important points consultations between the architect, draughtsmen, and client are necessary. In designing the elevations and arranging the lay-out of the plans a great amount of study is required before the ultimate and satisfactory result is attained. These details of design have to be studied and sketched sometimes repeatedly (often in perspective view), using a soft pencil of course, before arriving at an entirely satisfactory solution of the problem.

With the small amount of data given, it can readily be seen that much depends on the ability of the draughtsman to carry out his work rapidly and efficiently. He can only do this by having a thorough and broad understanding of the subject. *And above all, he must follow a definite system of drawing, blocking out the important points first,* and filling in the details afterwards, as shown in the following plates. This method is easier, quicker, and more comprehensive than the method adopted by some student-draughtsmen who early in the work labor over unimportant details, almost to the utter neglect of the more essential parts of the drawing.

In the following set of plates the student will proceed with the plans and elevations almost line for line the same as the professional draughtsman would do. This method should be used for working out all drawings whether for small or large

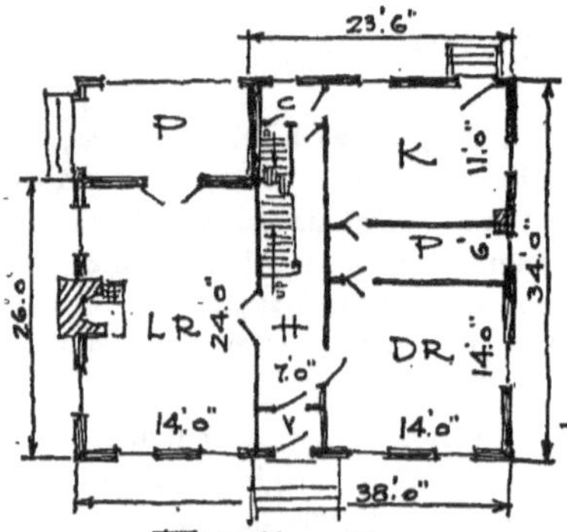

FIRST FLOOR PLAN

(23'6", 34'0", 38'0", 26'0")
- P
- K 11'0"
- P 6'0"
- L.R. 24'0" × 14'0"
- D.R. 14'0" × 14'0"
- H 7'0"

SECOND FLOOR PLAN

- ROOF
- B.R.
- B.R. 14'0"
- S.R. 7'0"
- B.R. 14'0"
- H 7'0"

FRONT ELEVATION

(7'6", 8'6", 9'0", 7'0")

L.R. 14' × 24'
D.R. 14' × 14'
K. 11' × 14'
P. 6' × 14'
H. 7'0" WIDE

9" BRICK – 4" HOLLOW TILE
SECOND STORY 9" BRICK
SECOND FLOOR
4 BED ROOMS
SEWING ROOM & BATH
ATTIC 2 BED ROOMS

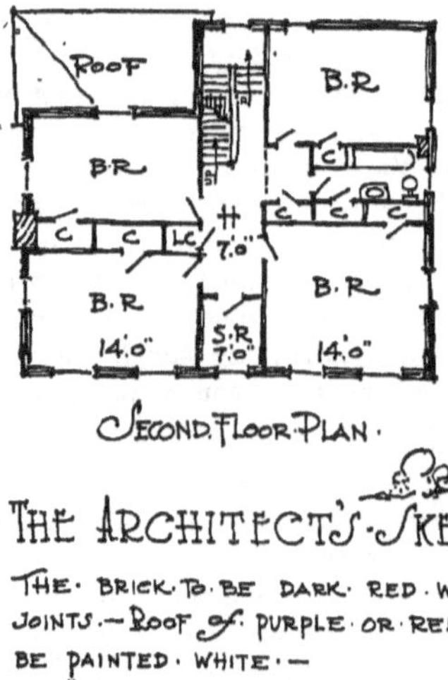

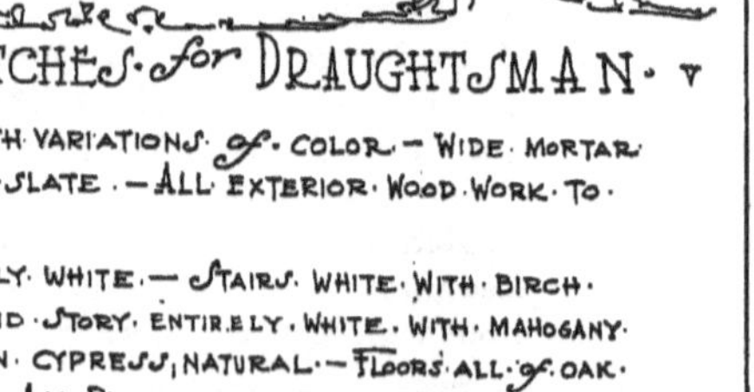

▽ THE ARCHITECT'S SKETCHES for DRAUGHTSMAN ▽

The brick to be dark red with variations of color. — Wide mortar joints. — Roof of purple or red slate. — All exterior wood work to be painted white. —

Finish of first story entirely white. — Stairs white with birch treads, newels & rails. — Second story entirely white with mahogany finish doors. — Attic finished in cypress, natural. — Floors all of oak.

Heating to be by hot water. — All plumbing fixtures porcelain. — Electric wiring by conduit system. — Gas in kitchen for range & water heater.

Plate 1.

buildings. The only differences are in the size, the arrangement of the rooms, the location of partitions, etc. All drawings should, of course, be first carefully drawn in lead pencil, and then just as carefully "inked in". Always cross the lines slightly at intersections even in inking, as shown throughout the plates in this book, and especially illustrated at the bottom of Plate 35.

In inking in a drawing the circles should be inked first, because better results are obtained by joining straight lines to curved ones than vice-versa. Next the horizontal lines should be inked, drawing from left to right and working from the top to the bottom of the paper. After the horizontal lines, the vertical lines should be inked. These are drawn from the bottom to the top of the paper, working from left to right. The freehand curves are inked after the other lines have been completed. The lettering should be inked in last.

PRACTICAL HINTS ON DRAWING

The student should first be certain that he is not drawing under unnecessary difficulties. He should have the light fall on his board unobstructed, from the front and left. He should see that his drawings and tools are within easy reach, and that he has a good scratch block, preferably fastened to the under side of his table or board with a cord. Avoid borrowing instruments. See that the T-square works easily along the edge of the board. Keep the drawing clean of pencil sharpenings, dust, etc., by the frequent use of a small dust brush.

In regard to work on the drawing itself, the student should keep his drawing pencil well sharpened to a long fine point, and turn it as the line is drawn to keep the point in good shape. The point should never be so short that the wood part of the pencil touches the T-square or triangle, as this results in a ragged line. Use a medium-soft pencil, HB, F, or H (No. 2, 3, or 4) in preference to an exceedingly hard pencil, as a drawing of much better character can be made with a soft pencil when kept well pointed, and the lines are much easier erased when not needed.

When laying out a drawing first determine its position on the sheet so that it will appear to the best advantage, taking future lettering and surrounding scale details or notes into consideration. Then determine the most important parts of the drawing and *put these in first*. Concise indication of the essential parts of a plan or elevation will help the progress of the drawing materially, and make the entire lay-out much more easily understood. After the essential or construction parts are drawn, the details may be worked in as hereafter shown.

Plans.—In drawing a plan the essential parts are the outside wall lines and the positions of the interior partitions, irrespective of doors, windows, etc. After the walls and partitions are indicated, the windows and doors, chimneys, stairs, dressers, fixtures, porches, and other details may be shown in their correct locations. In all the plans and elevations always work to *center lines* of windows, doors, and like details, instead of working to the sides of them. It is obvious that in this way the work can be laid out more rapidly and also more accurately than when working to side lines.

Room Sizes.—The sizes of rooms and their location will be determined by the requirements and the direction in which the building is to face. While there are no regular dimensions for the various rooms, certain standards will be suggested which may be helpful. The dimensions are often regulated by the quantity and position of the furniture, especially in the dining-room, kitchen, and in the bedrooms. In the living-room it is necessary to provide spaces for a piano, bookcases, and other furniture; in the dining-room about 6 feet of wall space is necessary for a sideboard, which is usually placed in the center of a side wall either towards the kitchen or directly opposite the main hall entrance to the room. The kitchen, of course, requires spaces for a sink with drain boards, dresser, coal and gas ranges and boiler, and also a good location for the work table. If possible, the bedrooms should have two places where a bed might be placed, and also spaces for dressers and dressing tables. All bedrooms should have ample closet space. The bathroom should have plenty of space for all fixtures, which should be placed to the best advantage for plumbing installation.

Most of the rooms should be rectangular in shape rather than square, in the proportion of about 14' to 16'. The living-room is often twice as long as it is wide. This is made necessary by its position on the plan, and by the requirements of the room. The various rooms and passages should be approximately the following sizes: the living-room from 14' x 16' to 18' x 30'; the dining-room, 14' x 14' or 13' x 15' to 16' x 20'; the hall at least 7' wide; pantry at least 6' wide; kitchen, 10' x 12' to 14' x 16'; bedrooms, 10' x 12' to 14' x 18'; bathrooms, 7' x 10' or more; passage halls, 3' wide or more. In large houses the above rooms are of course made as spacious as possible and may exceed the dimensions given, but these dimensions may be used as a standard, which may be altered by special requirements.

Walls.—The outside walls of brick houses and the smaller class of buildings are usually 9" or 13" thick, with 2" inside for furring and plastering, or they may be 9" brick and 4" hollow tile. Eight inch, 10" or 12" hollow tile walls, rough cast on the outside are also used. If the building is frame the outside wall will be 7" thick (2" x 4" stud, 1" sheathing, 1" outside finish, and 1" inside plastering). Interior partitions are 6" thick for main partitions and 4" or 6" for closet partitions.

Interior Details.—Door openings are 2'-8", 2'-10", or 3'-0" wide for main rooms, and 2'-4" or 2'-6" for closets. Double doors are 4'-0" to 5'-6" wide. Doors are 6'-8", 6'-10", 7'-0", or 7'-6" high. Outside doors are 3'-0" or 3'-2" wide, and 6'-10" to 7'-6" high, the use of a transom or over-door above being determined by the design. Stairs should be at least 3'-0" wide, wall to inside of rail, for the main stair, and 2'-6" in the clear for rear, cellar, and attic stairs. Treads should be 10" (rise to rise), and risers 7½" or slightly less for the main stair. Rear, cellar, and attic stairs may have 9" treads, and 8" or 8½" risers.

Chimney flues may be 8" x 8", 8" x 12", or 12" x 12". Some are made of terracotta, and require 4" or more of brick around them to strengthen and make them look sturdy in elevation.

Windows shown on a plan should be approximately 3'-2" wide, 3'-6" to 4'-0" wide if an outside architrave is used. The windows may vary considerably in order to obtain good proportions in the elevations, but sufficient wall space should always be left for furniture. Casement and other special windows are optional, depending on the effect desired.

Outside porch columns are usually .10″, 12″ or more in diameter for round columns, and 8″ to 10″ square for square columns. See Plates 20 and 21. Piers may be 12″ x 12″, 12″ x 17″, or any dimension which looks well in the design, and can be worked out in brick sizes. Porch steps are 12″ wide, and rails are 3″ wide.

Fixtures.—In indicating bathroom and kitchen fixtures in the plan, see Plate 8, use the following dimensions and directions: (1) Bathtub, 2′-3″ to 2′-6″ wide and from 4′-0″ to 6′-0″ long, with either square or rounded end. (2) Lavatory, 20″ x 24″, with an eliptical bowl and double lines at the back to indicate the integral back against the wall. (3) Closet, 15″ circular seat and 18″ x 5″ back or tank joined by straight lines, the entire projection from the wall 2′-2″. (4) Kitchen sink, 24″ x 30″, drawn with double lines, and with an 18″ x 24″ drain board at one end or both ends. (5) Coal range, 2′-6″ x 3′-0″. (6) Boiler, 12″ circle. (7) Gas range, 24″ x 36″. (8) Dresser, 12″ deep and 4′-0″, 4′-6″, 5′-0″, or 6′-0″ long. There is an added width of 6″ at the bottom for the counter shelf and drawers underneath. (9) Soil pipe, 6″ circle. (10) Wash tray, 24″ x 26″, drawn with double lines.

Elevations.—The usual heights for ceilings are as follows, though they may vary with the requirements of the particular job: First story, 9′-0″ or 9′-6″; Second story, 8′-6″ or 9′-0″; Cellar, 7′-0″ in the clear. Floor joists are 2″ x 10″, and are covered with 1″ rough flooring and 1″ finished flooring. The plaster on the ceilings is 1″ thick, making the total thickness of the floor 13″. Attic floor joists may be 2″ x 8″. All floor joists are set 16″ on centers so lath joints will "break" properly. Rafters are 2″ x 8″ or 2″ x 10″, set 24″ on centers. If they are to be plastered they must be cross-furred with strips set 16″ on centers. Timbers in stock sizes of larger dimensions are used for joists, etc., when required.

When it is desired to have the first floor set up several steps above the grade, the height of the floor line and top of water table should be 2′-8″ above the grade line. The floor may also be set just one step (6″) above the grade, and the cellar windows set down in areas.

Exterior Details.—The dimensions from the floor lines to window sills (top of outside masonry sill) should be approximately 2′-3″. The usual lengths of window panes for the first story are 28″, 30″, or 32″, making the openings 5′-6″, 5′-10″, or 6′-2″ in height if a 2″ reveal of frame is used, and higher if an especially wide architrave is used. The second-story windows usually have 26″ or 28″ glass, making the total height of the openings 5′-2″ or 5′-6″. Kitchen, pantry and bathroom window openings are usually less than stated above in order to have the sills set at a higher level. These dimensions are given as a guide for laying out work, and of course may vary slightly with peculiarities of design. Kitchen window sills are usually 3'-0" to 3'-6" above the floor line. This distance is to the top of the outside masonry sill. The widths of windows and doors was noted previously under the head of Plans. The usual heights of outside door openings are 6'-10", 7'-0", and 7'-6". In public buildings these may be made higher.

The window sills of masonry buildings are made of 5" or 7½" stone, or 4" brick set on edge, with a cement wash. Heads are of 7½", 10", or 12" stone; or brick ground to the proper radius; or 8" and 4" brick set on edge; or they are made of 8" or 12" brick segmental arches. All may have brick or stone key-stones and skew-blocks, according to design. These should project 2½" or 5" above the top of a flat arch, and if the cornice bed mould comes directly over the second story arches, either one or two courses of brick stretchers should show between the top of key block or arch and the bottom of the bed mould. Examples of window sills, heads, etc., will be found on Plate 18. The illustrations will help explain the above. Door openings have 5" or 6" stone sills.

Door and window openings of frame buildings usually have a 4" or 4½" plain or moulded outside architrave, and 2" wood sills.

Slate and wood shingle roofs, to be free from leaks, should have at least a 30 degree pitch, but seldom more than 45 degrees. Tin and slag roofs are kept flat, but with a pitch of not less than ¼" to the foot.

Show rafters or brackets are spaced approximately 24" on centers. Porch floors should be 3" to 6" below the floor of the house. Porch rails are approximately 2'-6" high. Columns and steps have been previously noted under the head of Plans. The height of porches should be 8'-0" to 9'-6" from the floor to the under side of the plate or cornice soffit. Water tables are of stone, or brick on edge, about 8" to 12" in height. In frame structures they are of wood.

PROGRESSIVE STEPS IN THE DEVELOPMENT OF PLANS

Carefully study Plate 8, and use the information shown there when drawing plans at ¼" scale.

(1)—First draw the front and rear walls and indicate the parallel inside partitions in their correct positions. In this plan the outside walls should be 13", 9" for the brick and 4" for hollow tile. The inside stud partitions are 6" thick. The length of the lines should be indefinite, but approximately the width of building.

(2)—Draw the side-wall lines and indicate the hall partitions, and any other partitions parallel to them. These partitions should also be drawn with lines of indefinite length.

(3)—All the partitions are next drawn their entire lengths, irrespective of the position of doors, etc.

(4)—Indicate the positions and correct widths of the inside doors, locating them by center lines when coming on the axes of rooms or halls. Locate and outline the fireplace and chimney flues. The brick column of the rear porch is located.

(5)—Erase partition lines in the inside door openings, and show which way the doors swing. Draw the center lines and indicate the widths for all window and outside door openings. The stairs must be figured out and drawn according to the heights of ceilings and the number of steps. Consult Plate 9. This applies to the main and cellar stairs. A broken line separates them. Draw the 4" x 4" tiles of the hearth for the fireplace. Letter the rooms, halls and porch uniformly and of a size that is "in scale" with the entire drawing. Study Plates 35 and 36 for architectural lettering.

(6)—Draw the outside steps. The window and door openings should have the frames drawn according to the style determined upon. See Plate 8. Complete the drawing of the plan of the fireplace, following the details shown on Plate 8. The radiators are shown in their correct locations. Their sizes and heights should be indicated by lettering. Electric and gas outlets should likewise be shown in their correct locations. Switches should be located with an "S," and dotted lines drawn from the switches to the electric lights. The number of lights at each outlet should also be shown. Draw the fixtures of the kitchen and pantry according to the plan details shown on Plate 8.

Draw the line in the outside walls which indicates that brick and hollow tile are used. The line should be 4" from the inside edge of the wall. Indicate different materials by cross-hatching.

STEPS IN THE DEVELOPMENT OF PLANS

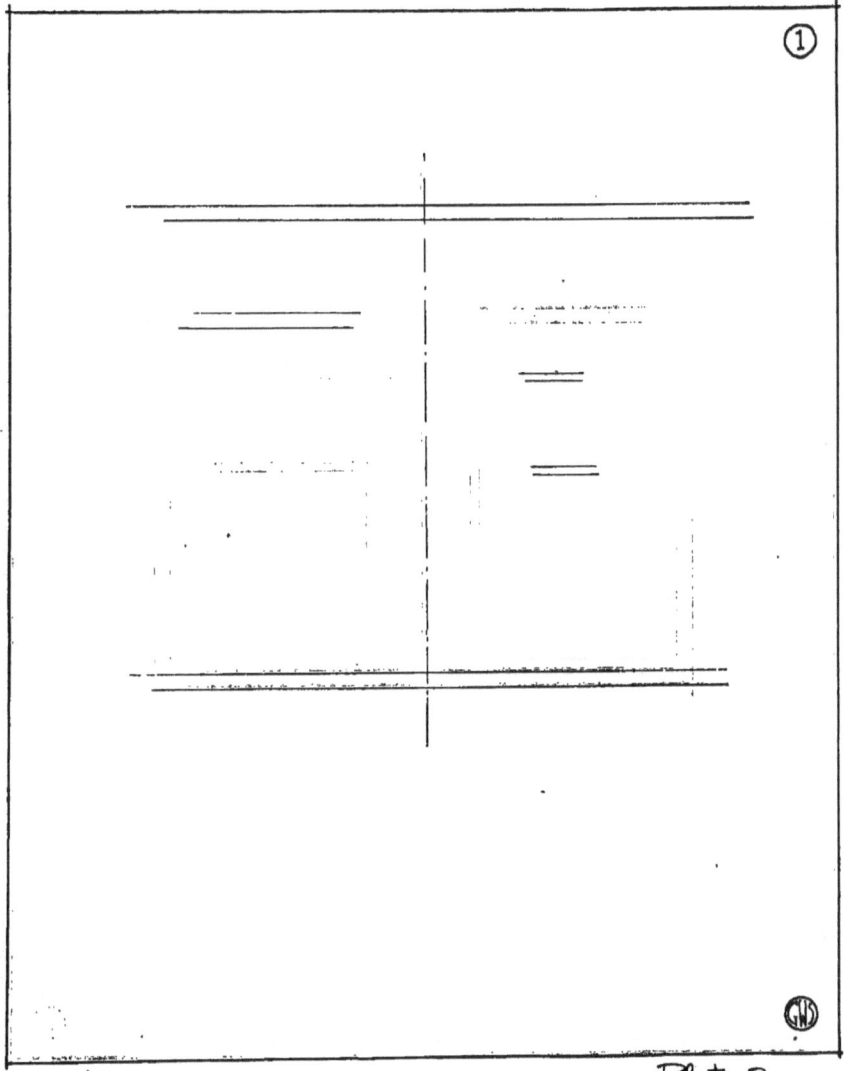

Plate 2

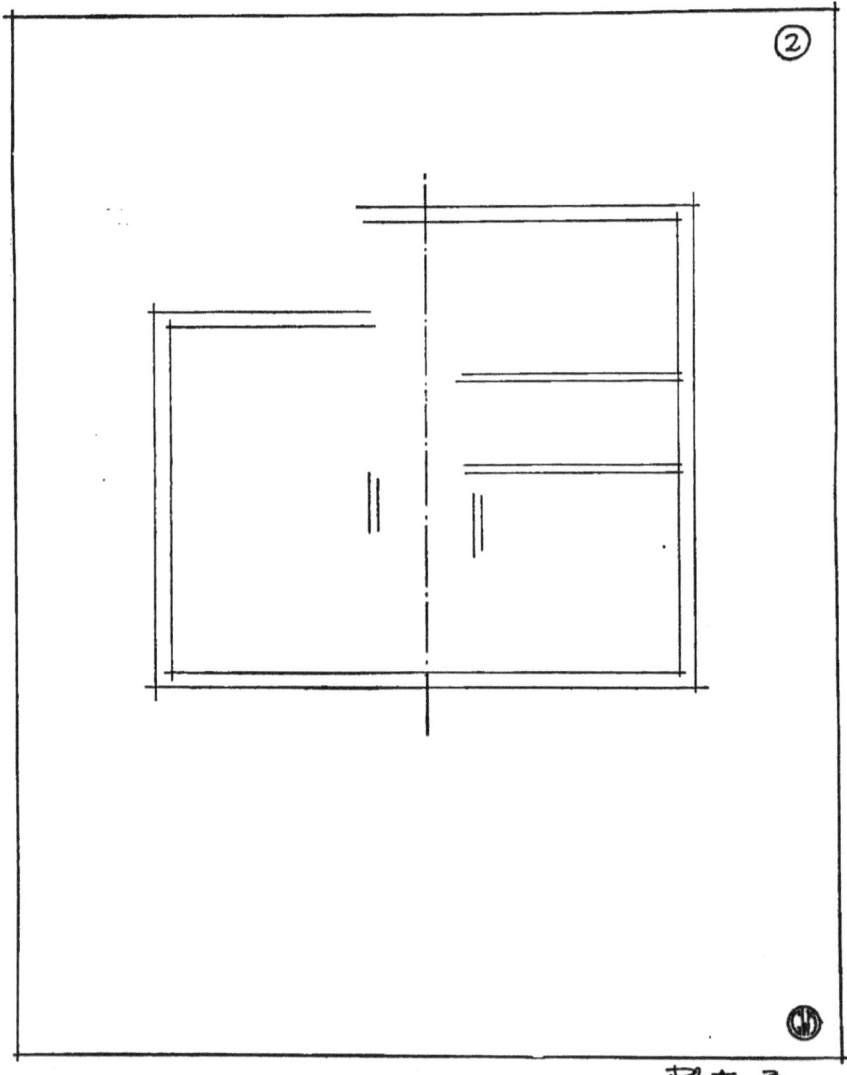

Plate 3

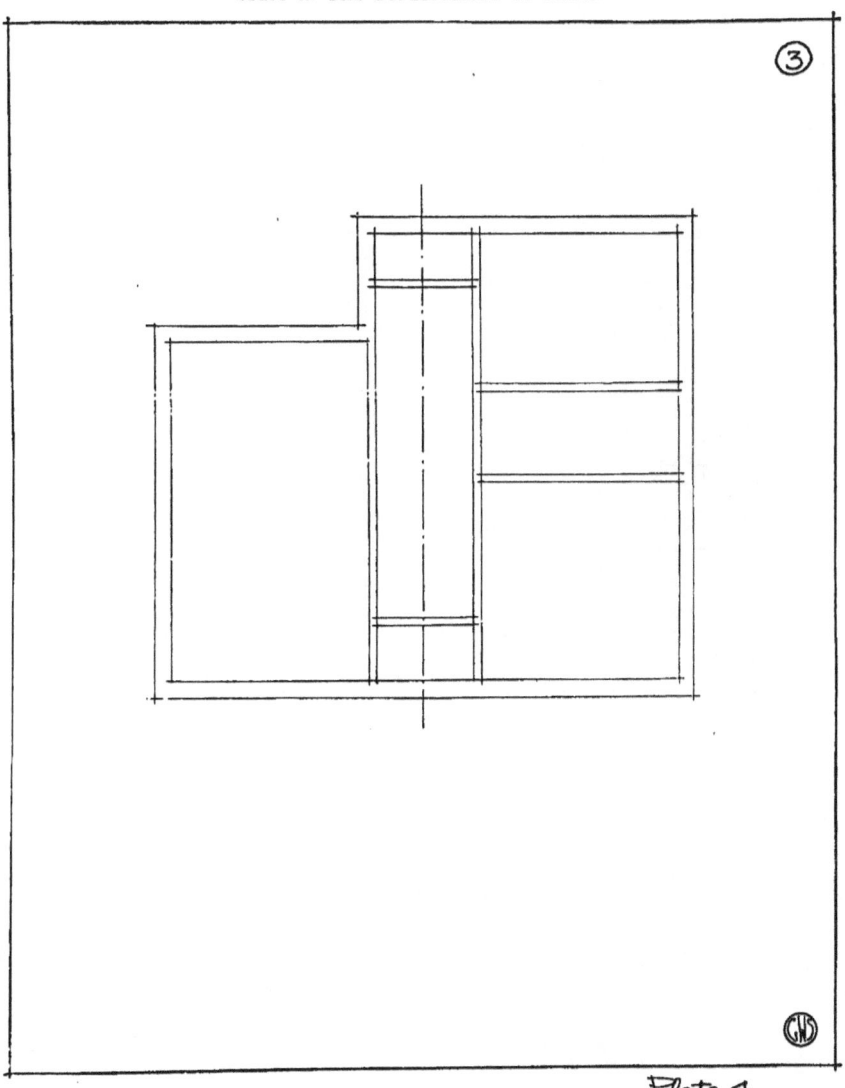

Plate 4

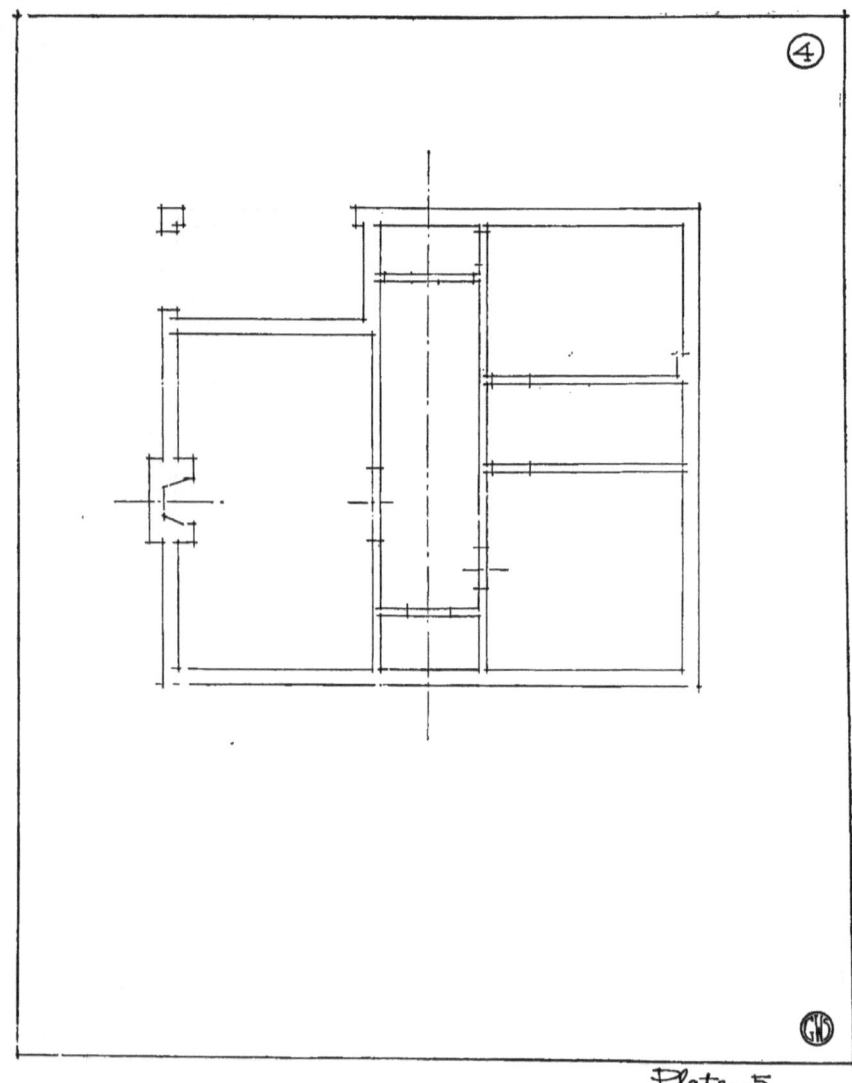

Plate 5

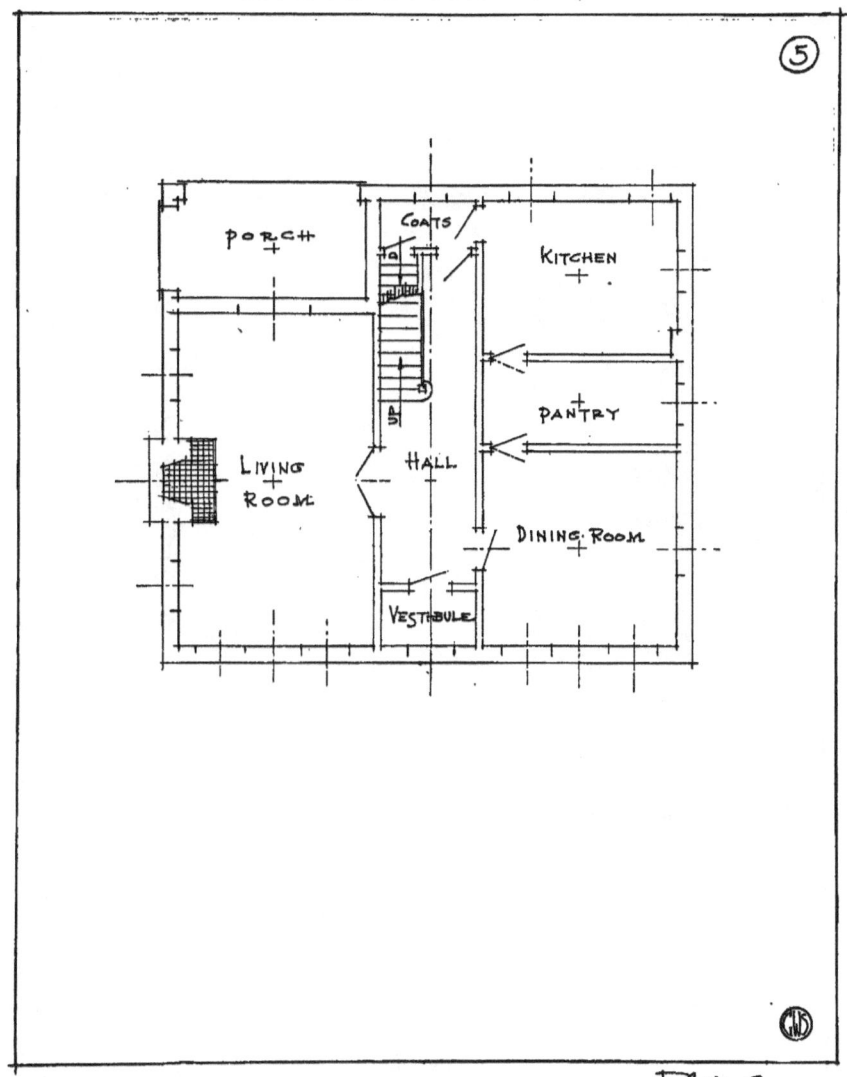

Plate 6

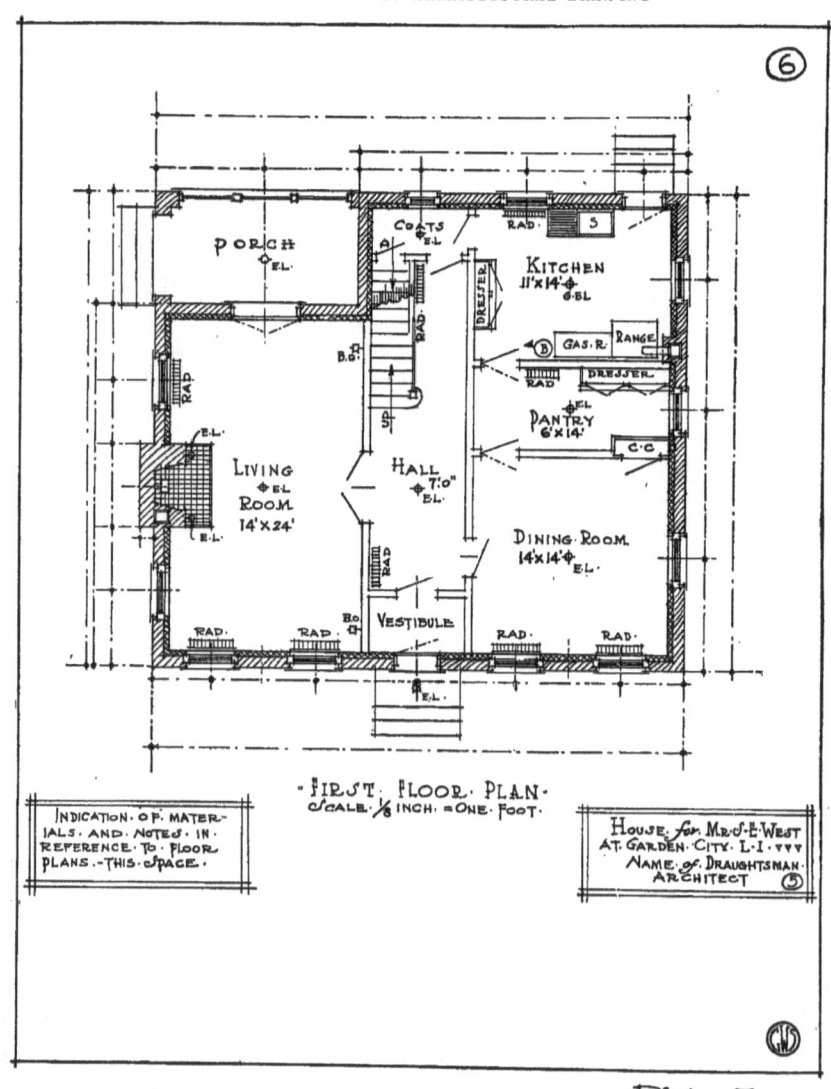

Draw the exterior over-all dimension lines, and also the subordinate dimension lines locating the window and door openings and the projections or breaks in the wall surfaces in the plan. All openings are dimensioned to centers. Use arrow heads or heavy dots for the intersections and ends of dimension lines. Also run a dimension line through the plan in each direction, locating the main partitions of the building; the dimensions being taken between the bare construction of the brick walls and stud surfaces irrespective of furring or plaster. These dimensions determine the size of the rooms, halls, etc.

Letter in the title of the plan, scale, indication of materials, name of owner, and architect's name as indicated. Letter any fixtures requiring it, and also mark the sizes of interior doors.

The drawing is now ready to ink. Follow the rules previously given for the order of inking the lines. Ink in the full lines first. Use light lines for inking the projection and dimension lines, the cross-hatching of the brick and hollow tile, and for the radiators.

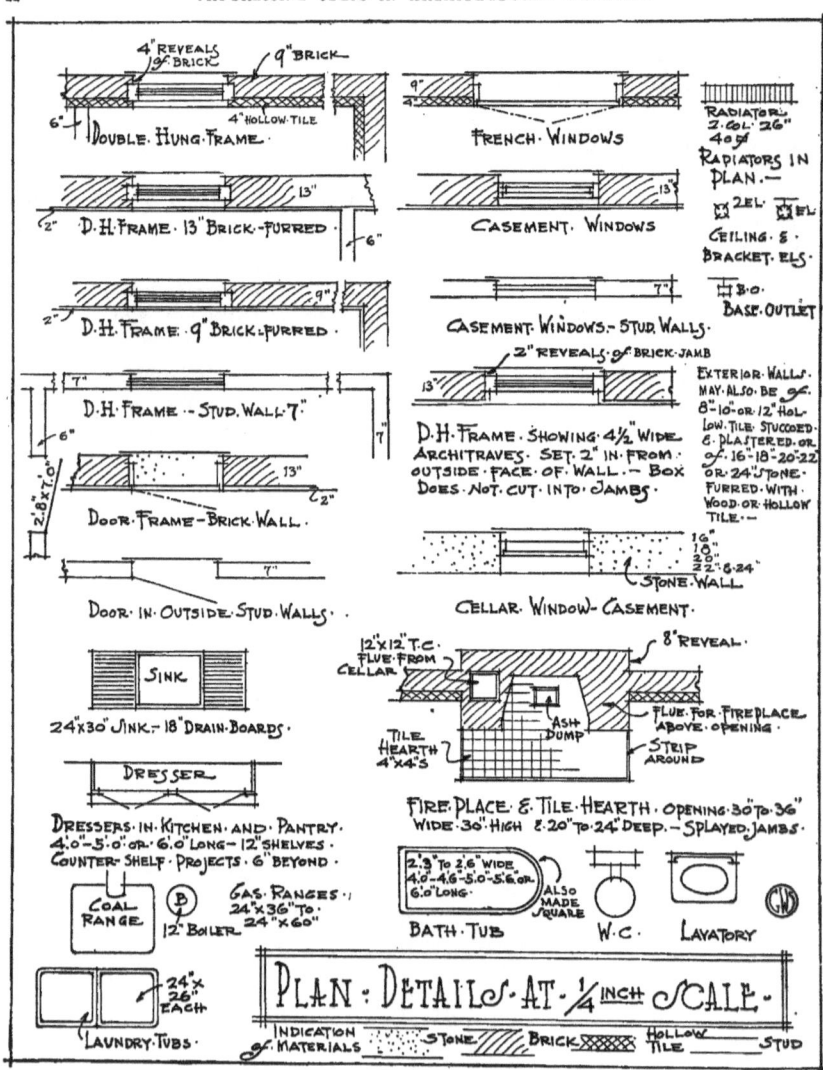

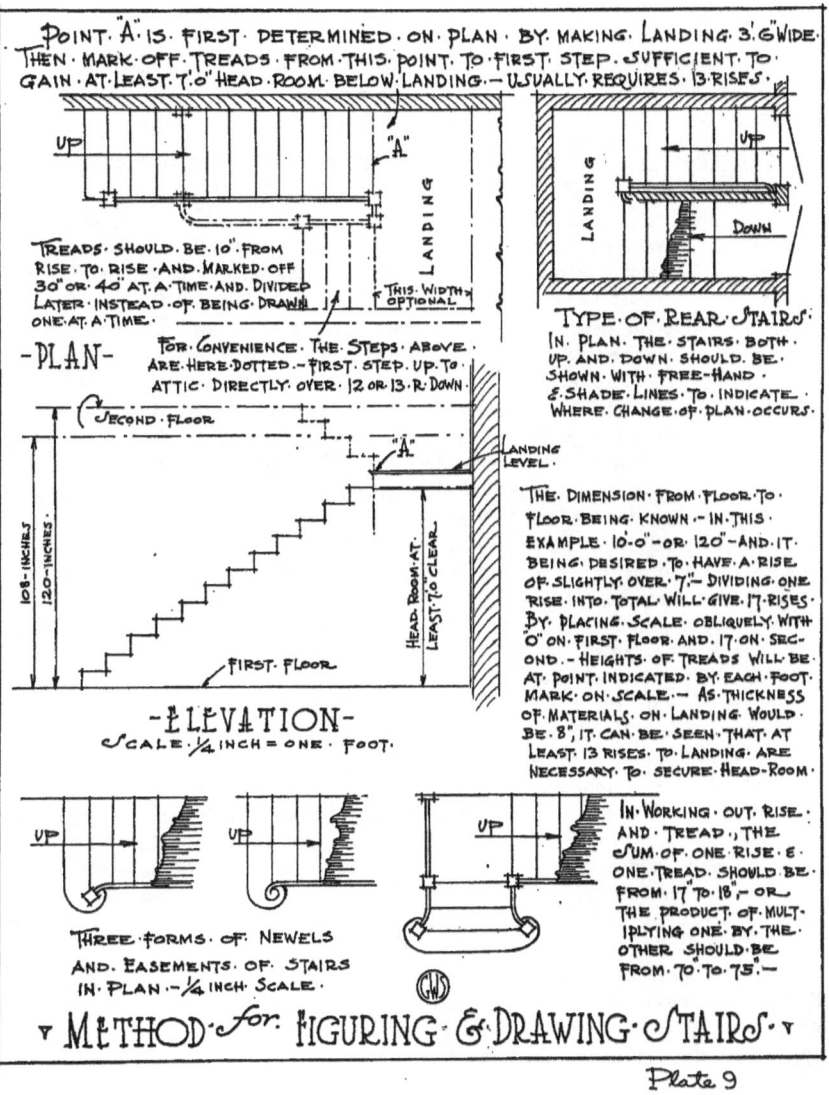

PROGRESSIVE STEPS IN THE DEVELOPMENT OF ELEVATIONS

Carefully study, and refer when necessary, to Plates 16 to 21, inclusive, when drawing elevations at ¼" scale.

These progressive steps are to be observed and *followed,* not only in this elevation, but in every elevation worked out. The size and details may vary with the design, but the method of constructing the working drawing should always be the same, in order to facilitate the work and get the best results.

(1)—Draw the grade or base line first. Keep the line up high enough on the sheet to allow for the title and lettering below and the entire height of the finished elevation above. Do not start the drawing with roofs or cornices or side lines.

(2)—Draw the lines indicating the main corners of the building. Then draw the height of the water table and mark the story heights at the side of the elevation, and from these story marks draw lines lightly through the building.

(3)—The cornice and roof are then blocked out with light lines. The pitch and shape of the roof are determined by the design and effect desired, and should work out correctly with the width of the side elevation and the height of the ridge line. The positions of the main cornice lines are determined by the construction, as worked out at the plate and the foot of the rafters. Approximately, the top cornice line should be about level with the top of the attic floor joists. The detail lines and the profile of the cornice mouldings, brackets, etc., are to be worked out later. As previously indicated, the roof seldom has less than a 30 degree or more than a 45 degree pitch, if covered with slate or wood shingles. These have a tendency to leak if laid on a pitch of less than 30 degrees. Only the main lines of the cornice should be worked out at this time.

(4)—Get measurements of all vertical lines, such as corners, window and door jambs and centers, chimneys, etc., from the plan, "ticking" them off accurately with a strip of paper. Transfer them to the elevation and draw the side lines of the chimneys and window and door openings. Draw these lines of indefinite length. Draw in the center lines lightly for all openings. These center lines will be found of great help later in working out the details of the windows and doors, and also maintain "balance" in the design and details.

(5)—A projecting band of brick, which is optional, is shown at the second floor level. Draw the heads and sills of the window and door openings. The heights of these are determined by the design and effect desired. The sills are approximately 2'-3" from the floor line to the top of the outside sill. The heights

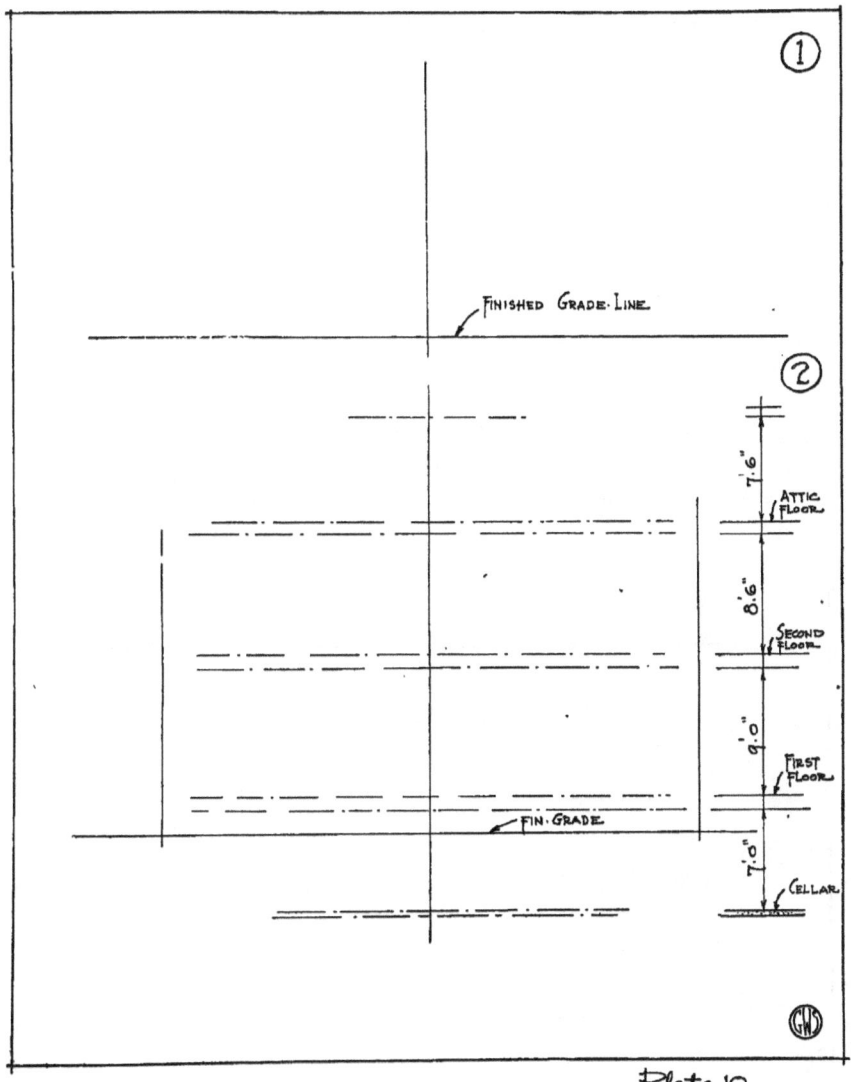

Plate 10

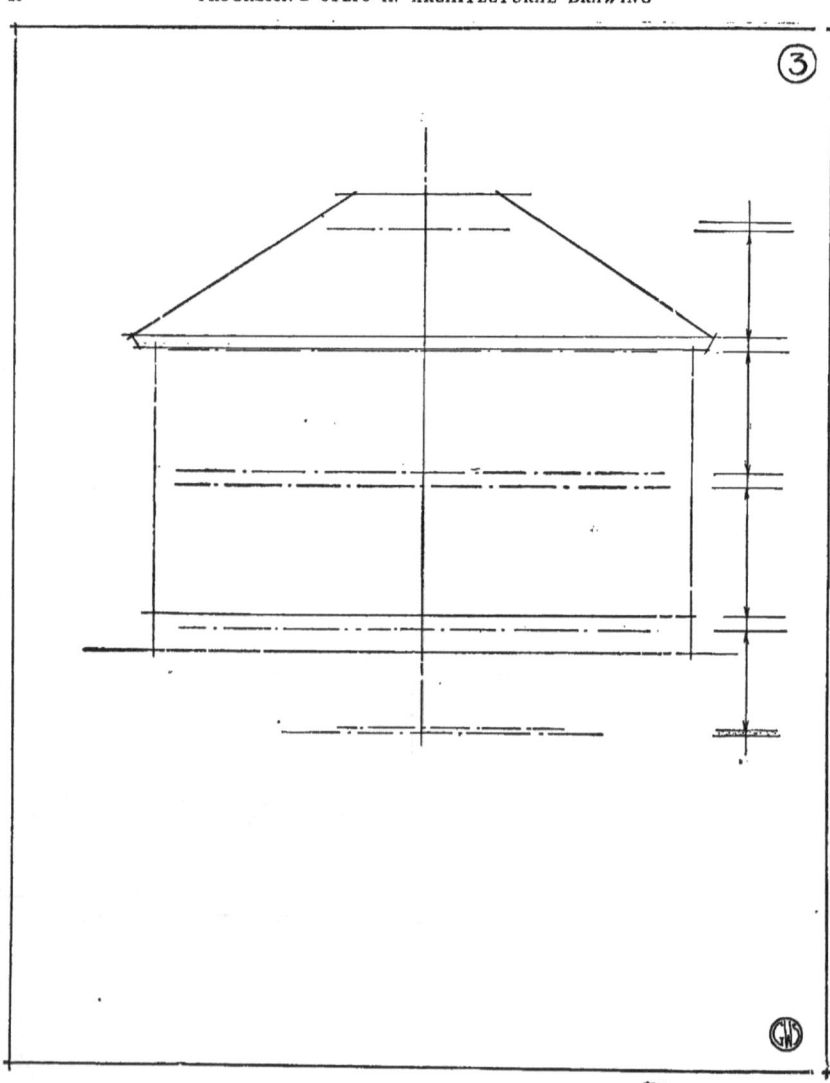

Plate 11

STEPS IN THE DEVELOPMENT OF ELEVATIONS

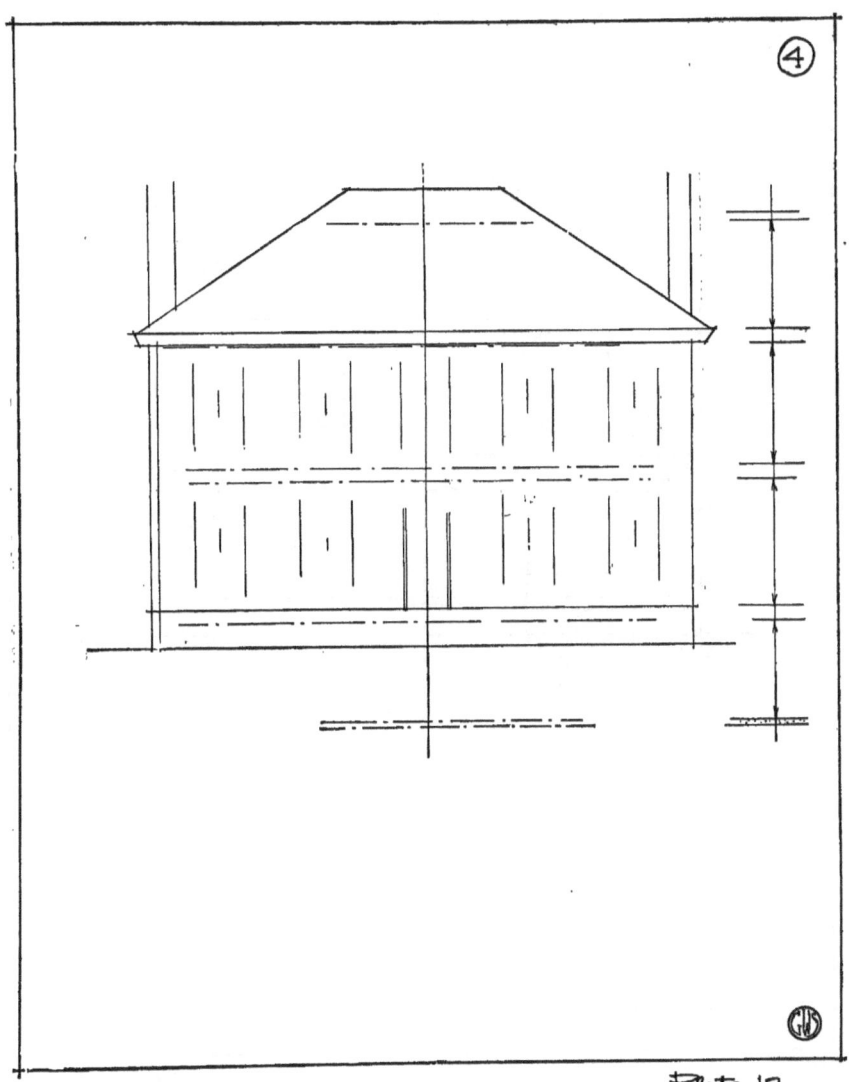

Plate 12

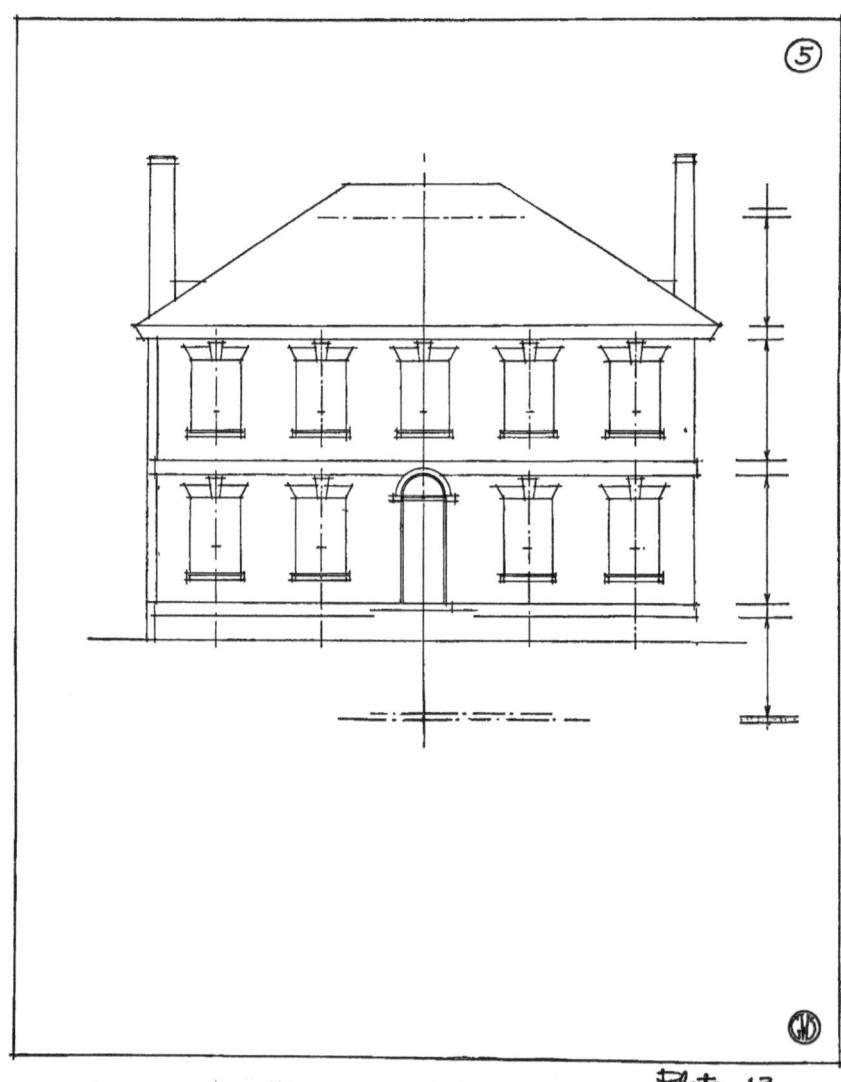

Plate 13

STEPS IN THE DEVELOPMENT OF ELEVATIONS

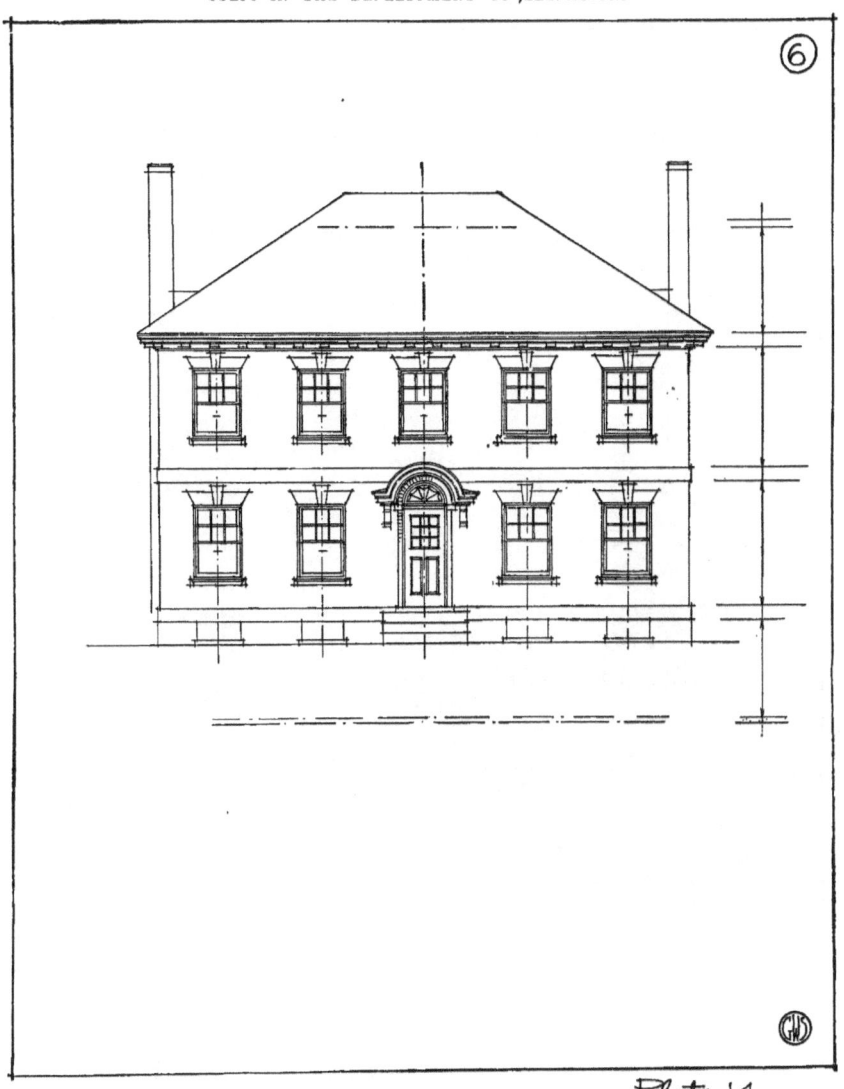

Plate 14

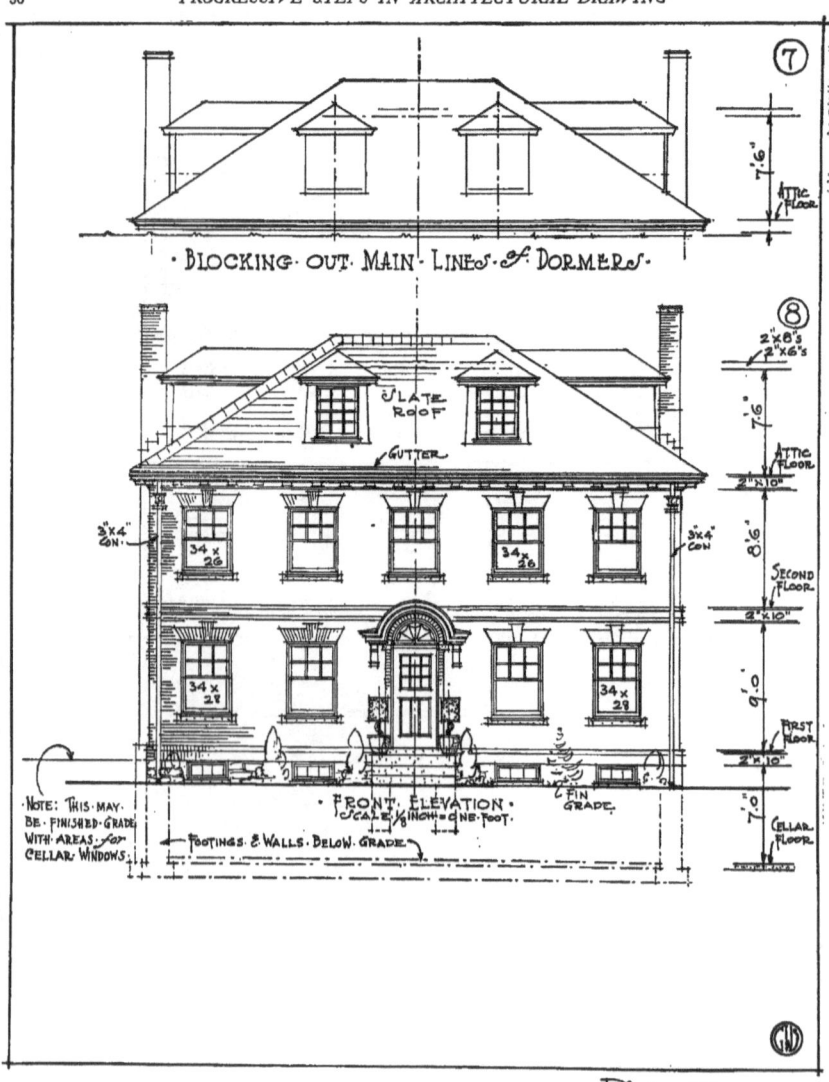

of openings of the windows should approximate 5'-6" for the first story, and 5'-0" for the second story, though these dimensions may vary slightly. Draw in the details of the window heads, using Plate 18 for reference. In this example 10" or 12" ground brick flat arches and key stones 2½" or 5" higher, are used. The method of getting the radius centers is also shown on Plate 18. Indicate whether the chimney caps are of stone, brick or terra-cotta. They should be shown as uniformly as possible. Draw the gusset boards where the chimneys and roof intersect.

(6)—Draw the cornice profiles and moulding lines clearly, according to the particular style of cornice determined upon, and draw the modillions or brackets. These are from 16" to 24" or more on centers, usually 24", with the end modillion center line coming on the corner wall-line. The spaces, center to center, may have to be adjusted to divide the length evenly. Draw the bed mould below the modillions. Cornice profiles and details are shown on Plates 16 and 17.

The lines of window frames, sash and muntins are next drawn, and the door head and door worked out according to design. When used in masonry walls, the usual thickness or "reveal" of a door frame or window frame is 2" from the side face of the opening. The sash shows an additional 2" at the side. A single line at ¼" scale indicates each of these surfaces. Draw the wood sill 2" (double line to show wash), the lower sash rail 3", and meeting rail and muntins 1" in width. Any peculiarity of design in frames and sash will have to be specially detailed.

(7.)—The dormer windows should now be blocked out with side lines and the roof and cornice lines, all of which should be of a size and shape to be in harmony with the plan, and in correct proportion and style to harmonize with the elevations. Draw the side elevations of the dormers which front on the side elevation of the house, carrying the cornice lines, etc., across from the front. The bottom or sill line is regulated in height by the point where the front face of the dormer strikes the sloping roof in the side view. Consult Plate 19.

(8)—Draw the mouldings and modillions or brackets of the dormers and cornice. The frame, sash, and the muntin lines are then drawn for the dormer windows. Draw the cellar window frames and sash. Brick lines and stone indication may now be put in, but sparingly and well placed.

All descriptive lines of the elevation have now been completed. Such notes as are necessary should be neatly and carefully lettered, the lettering to be in proportion, uniform in height and style, and placed on the drawing in positions to look well. Make note of the brick and stone, frame, slate, shingle or tin roofs, hanging or box gutters and conductors, size of glass, and grade and floor lines. Repeat the notes only where necessary.

VARIATIONS IN PLANS AND ELEVATIONS

To simplify the explanation, the plan and elevation have been shown as direct and simple as possible. Certain variations in both plan and elevation might be suggested as adding interest to the problem. For example, in the plan a rear stair may be added by enlarging the area of the plan, and the pantry might possibly be rearranged in such a way as to get a coat closet from the hall by placing the passage doors to the kitchen near the outside wall. This would reverse the location of the china closet, and also require a change in the location of the kitchen range and chimney. An entry with a cold closet and space for a refrigerator might also be added to the kitchen.

These are, however, details which may be incorporated in the plan at the option of the draughtsman or may be made necessary by the requirements of the client.

The porch, or an open terrace, may be located at the side of the house instead of at the rear, with French windows leading to it from the living-room. The fireplace may perhaps be at the end rather than at the side of the living-room, with built-in bookcases and windows over them, at either side. This location for the chimney would not look so well on the elevation as it is in the position shown.

In the elevation, the front entrance door and the dormer windows could have variations. For instance, the door might have a pilastered and columned entrance, with either a pediment head, or a frieze and cornice with a wrought iron railing over it. The dormers might be made with a pediment, or a segment head. The main roof might be gabled at the ends, with either a wood cornice, or a brick parapet with a cut stone coping on the rake, instead of the hip roof as shown.

The height of the chimneys should be either level with the ridge of the roof, or slightly above that. The living-room chimney at the side should be stepped back with weatherings of stone, and the location of the side dormer arranged to allow as much space as possible between the dormer cornice and the chimney.

ELEVATIONS OF CORNICES AND CHIMNEYS

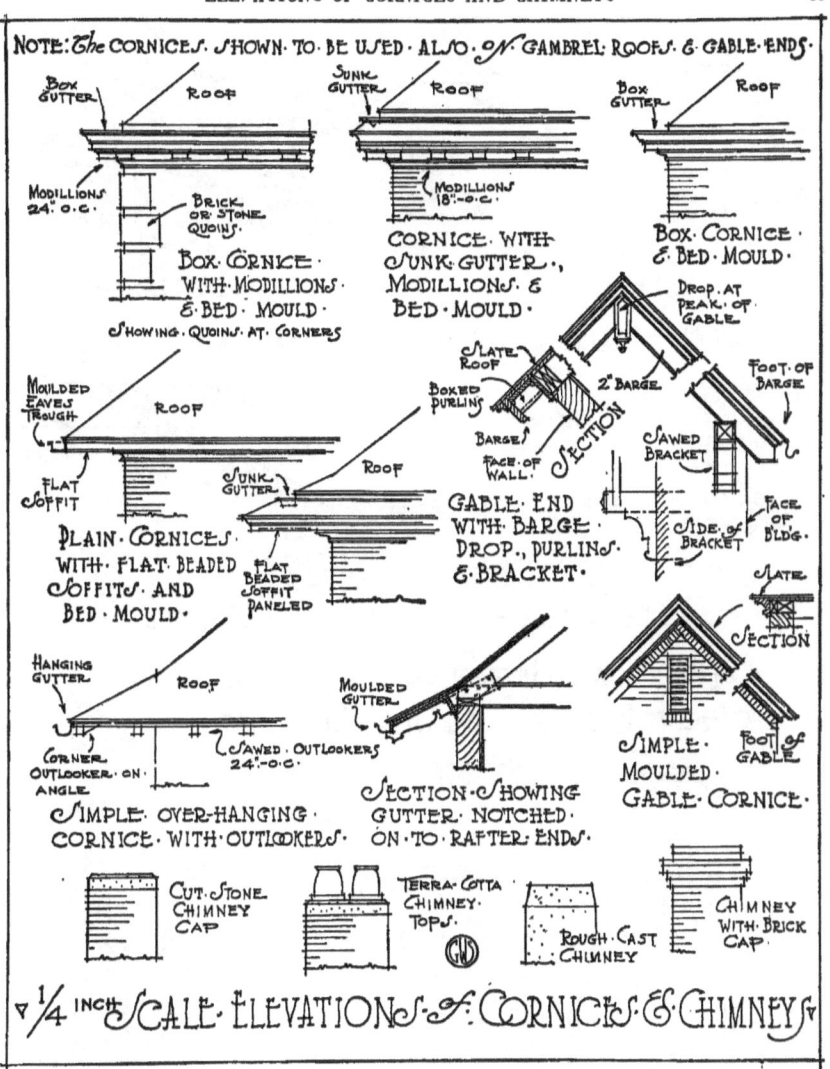

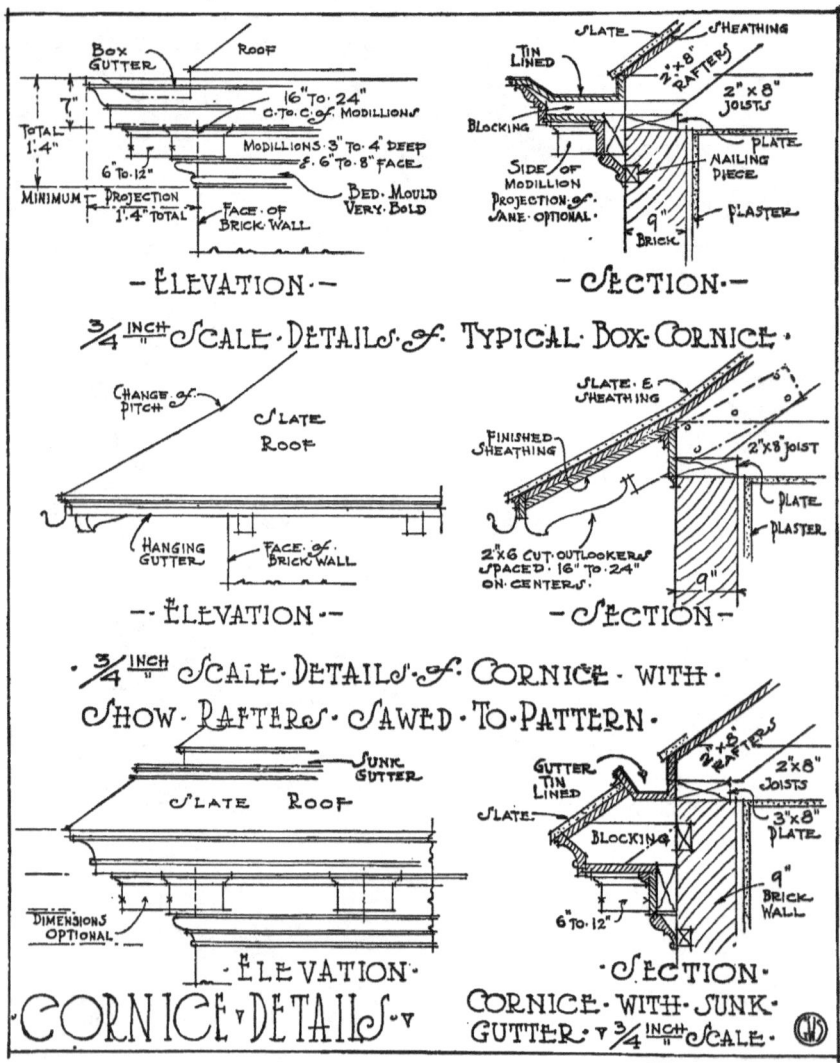

ELEVATIONS OF MASONRY WINDOW HEADS AND SILLS

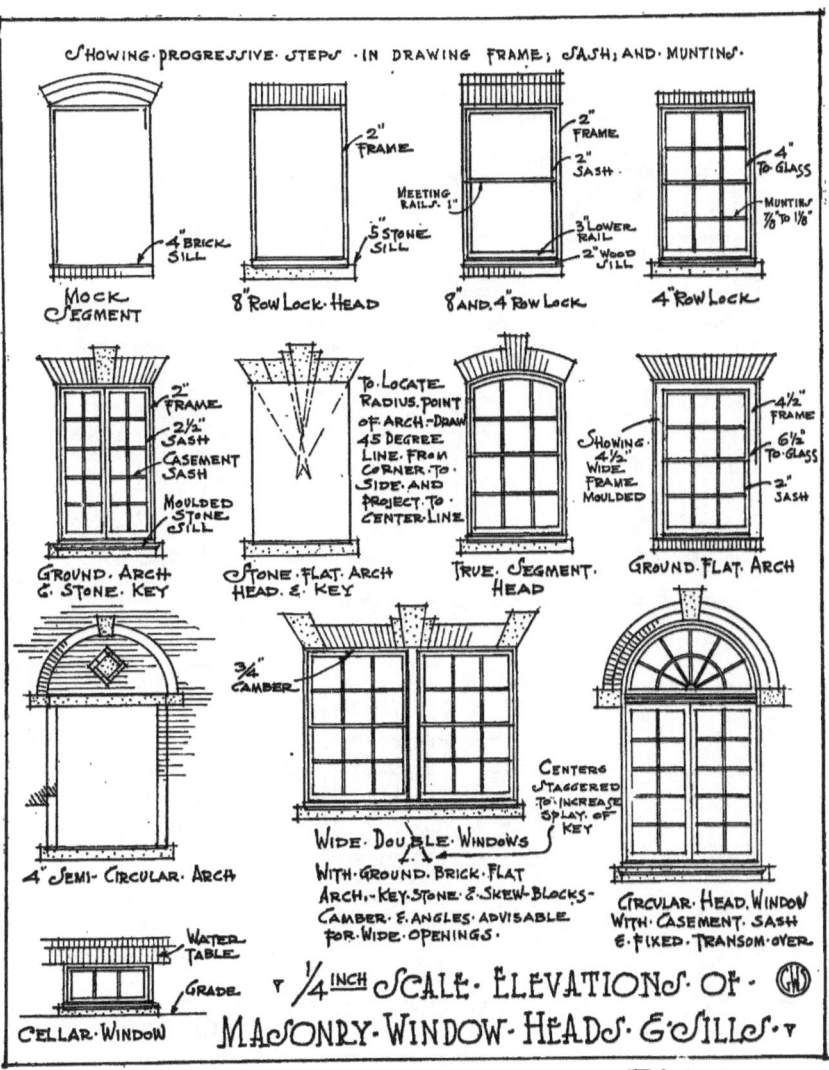

Plate 18

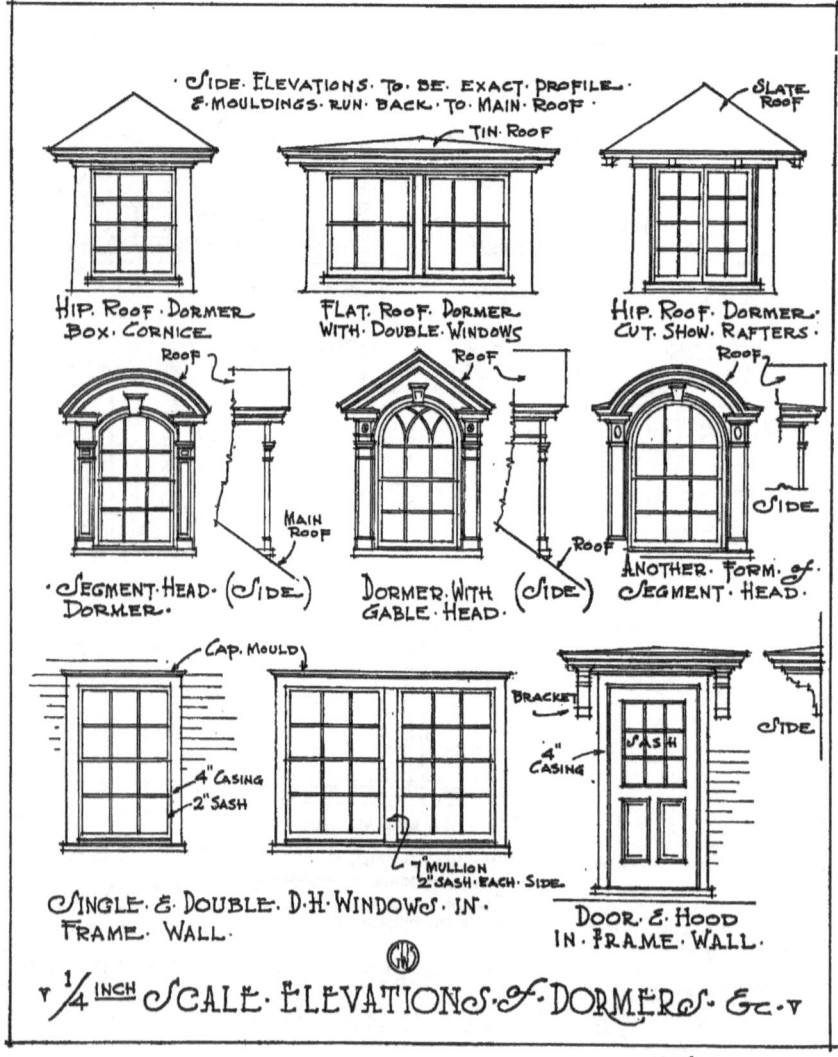

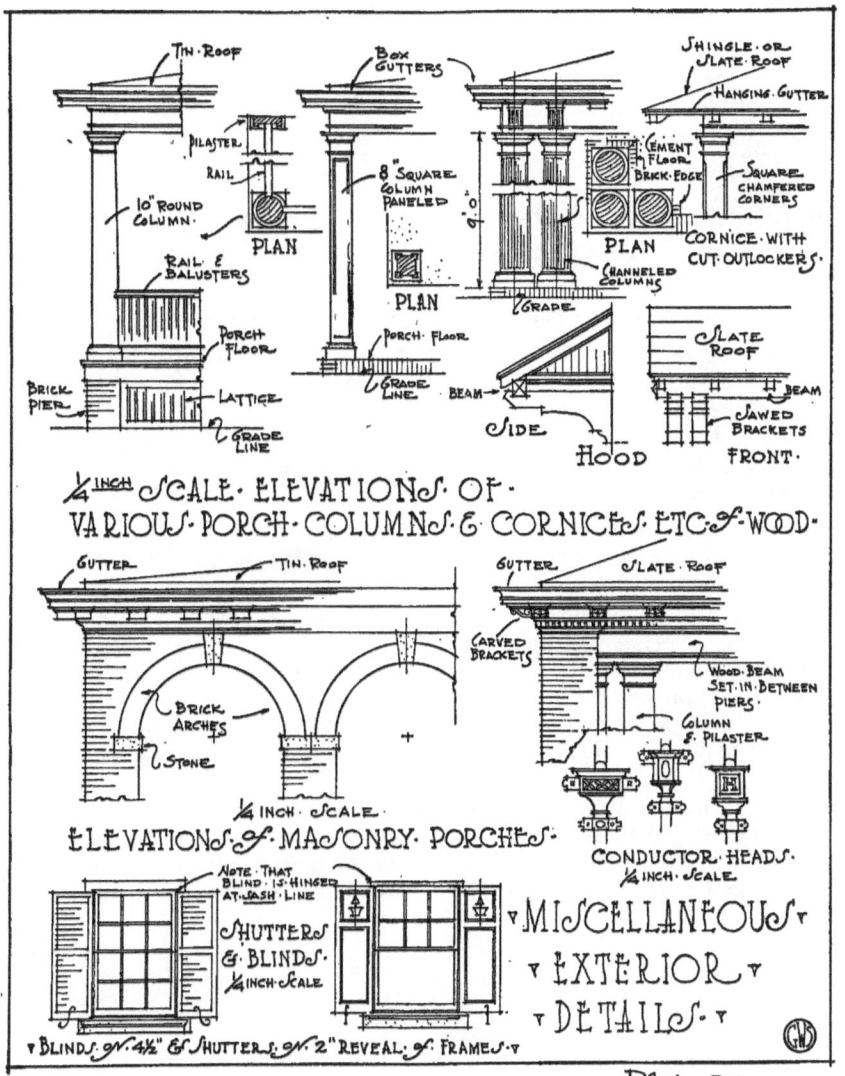

PROGRESSIVE STEPS IN THE DRAWING OF CORNICES ON ONE-QUARTER INCH SCALE ELEVATIONS

(1)—Draw the line indicating the main corner of the building.

(2)—Draw the top and bottom lines of the cornice proper, the height of which is determined in working out the details at the plate and foot of the rafter. The depth of this cornice in a house of ordinary size should be about 6" or 7".

(3)—Draw the lines indicating the mouldings in the cornice proper. The exact position of these lines is determined by the draughtsman's knowledge of the profile desired for the cornice.

(4)—Draw the profile clearly and the lines indicating the bed mould and facia at the back of the modillions. These are determined by the draughtsman's knowledge of proportion in cornice work.

(5)—The end modillion on the front elevation and the side of the first modillion on the side elevation should be drawn. Draw the profiles of the bed mould. The center line of the end modillion is approximately on an axis with the corner line of the building. Draw center lines for all modillions, approximately 24" on centers. If these do not space evenly, the distance from center to center should be adjusted so that they will. The uniform distance between centers may vary with the design.

(6)—Draw all side lines of the modillions, and then lines indicating the bottoms of them. Draw in the lines indicating the profile of the moulding at the intersection of the same with the under side of the cornice. When the members of mouldings are very small the profile is indicated by a line showing the general shape of the moulding.

STEPS IN DRAWING MAIN AND PORCH CORNICES, AND COLUMNS

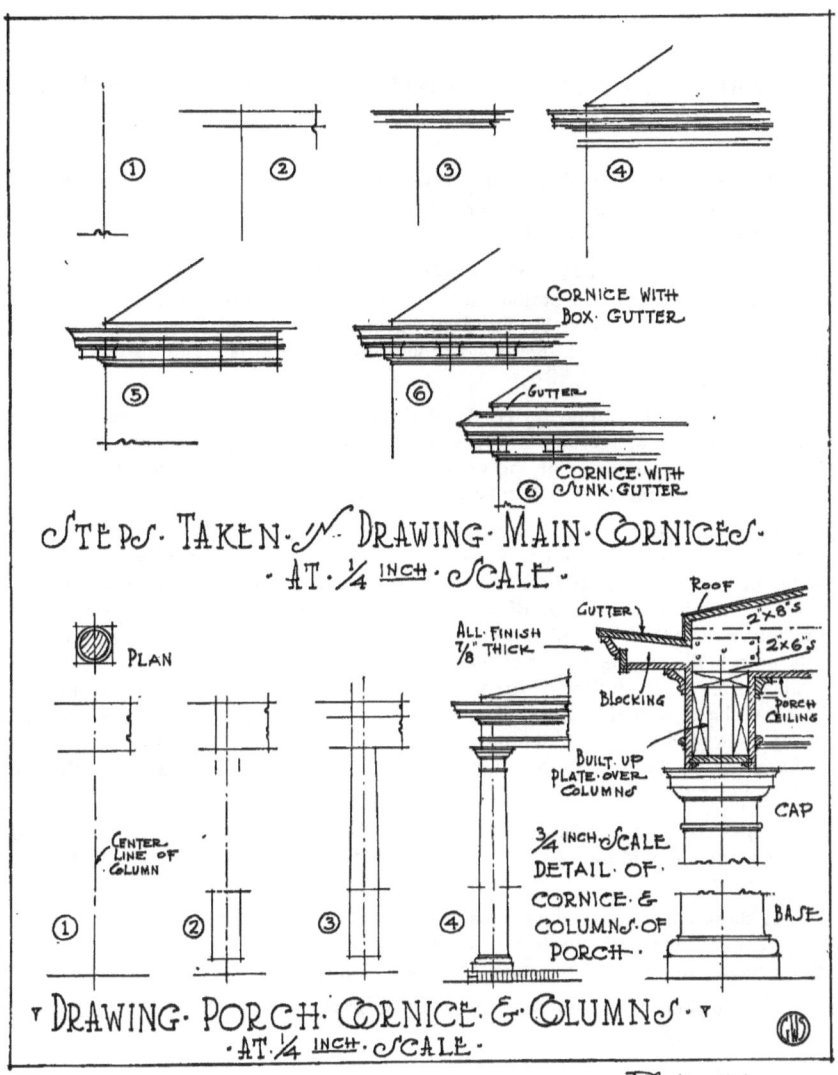

Plate 21

PROGRESSIVE STEPS IN THE DRAWING OF PORCH CORNICES AND COLUMNS AT ONE-QUARTER INCH SCALE

(1)—From the plan "tick off" accurately with a strip of paper the corners of the building and the center lines of all columns. Then draw the center lines in their correct locations, Plate 21.

(2)—Indicate the width of the column according to the desired proportions. Also indicate the top and bottom lines of the entablature over the column. The dimensions are determined by the draughtsman's knowledge of the height the column and entablature should be to have the proper proportions, and also by requirements of location, etc.

Draw lines indicating the frieze of the cornice. These should come directly over the necks of the columns. Draw in the line indicating the height of the base (one-half of the diameter of the column), and another line at one-third of the height of the column which is where the entasis begins.

(3)—One-third of the column is drawn straight, and the lines from this point to the cap have a gradual taper or entasis. The width at the neck should be five-sixths of the width at the base. This entasis is drawn properly by starting with the pencil point close to the edge of the triangle, then gradually sloping the pencil so the line will extend beyond the edge of the triangle at the center, and gradually returning to the edge as the other end is reached. This produces a very slight curve, which forms a true outline of the upper two-thirds of the column. The point should be very sharp, and the entasis drawn accurately in regard to width and balance. Draw a line indicating the depth of the cornice proper, the location of which is determined by the draughtsman's knowledge of proportion. The depth of this cornice would be approximately 5" or 6".

(4)—A line should be drawn indicating the roof and gutter. The profile lines of the cornice mouldings, and cap, necking, and base of the column should be carefully drawn.

A thorough study of the orders of architecture, and of the mouldings and fascias in connection with cornices is imperative before the draughtsman can expect to draw these profiles with any degree of spirit and certainty.

For further study and reference consult Plates 16, 17, 20, 25, 26, 31, 32, 33 and 34.

DETAILS OF WINDOW AND DOOR FRAMES

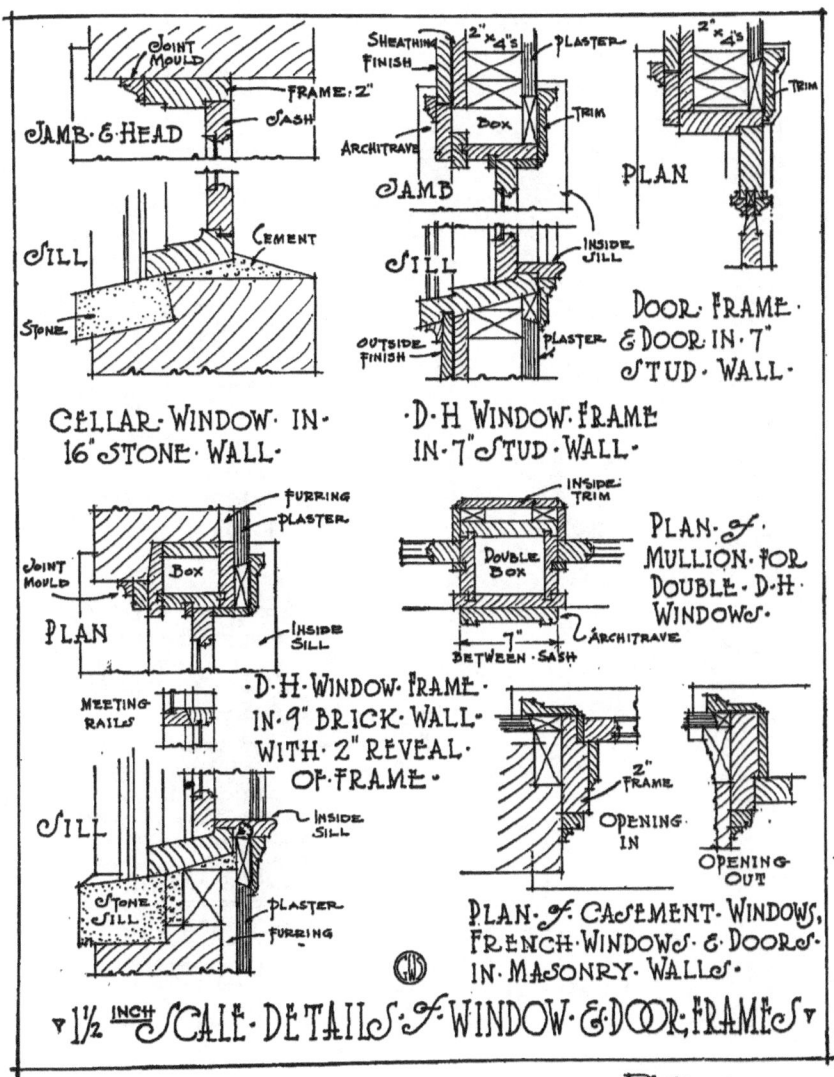

Plate 22

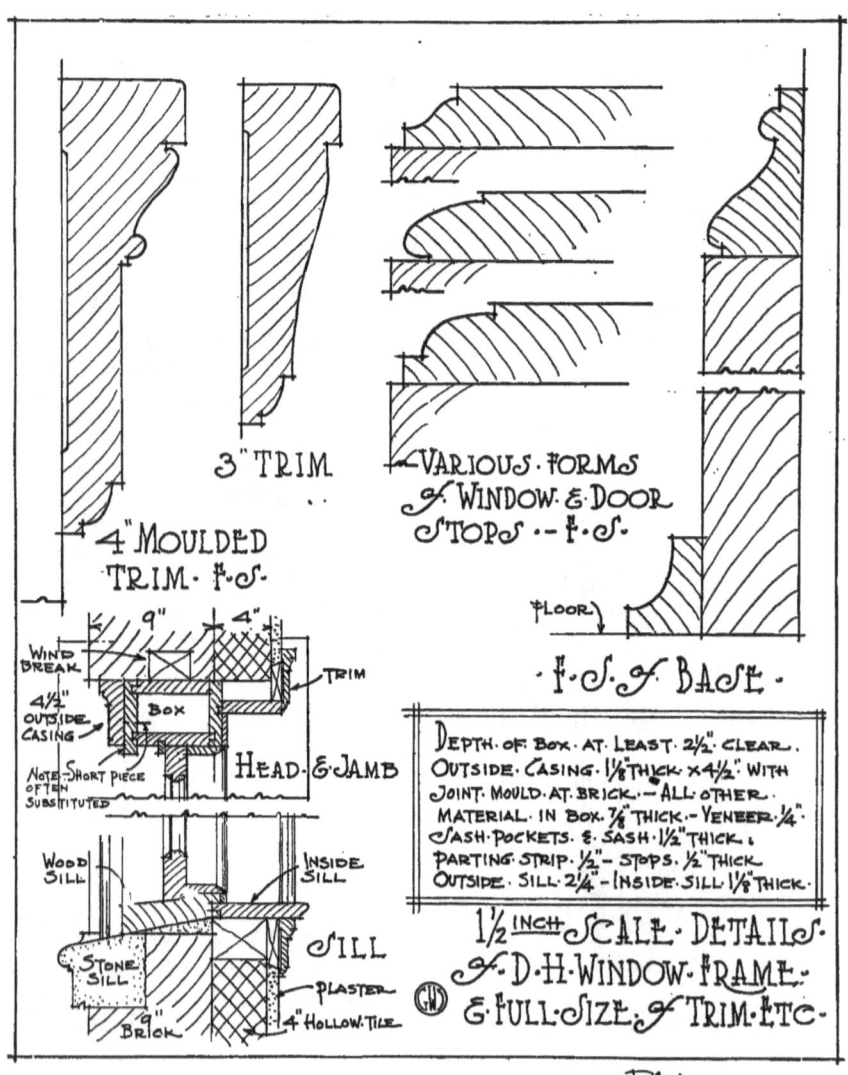

PROGRESSIVE STEPS IN DRAWING DETAILS OF DOUBLE-HUNG WINDOW FRAMES AT SCALE OR FULL SIZE

(1)—The width of the wall at the jamb is first indicated; and furring and plaster lines are shown, Plate 24.

(2)—The main lay-out of the window-box is drawn. All material should be ⅞" thick except the outside casing, which is ⅝" and formed to receive the shutter. The 2" reveal of the frame set in the brick wall is shown. The outside lining sets back 4" from the face of the wall and the 1⅛" outside casing and joint mould are nailed to the outside of the frame. The outside face of the pulley stile should be shown 2" from the brick jamb, and the depth inside the box is about 2½" so the weights can work freely. With the pulley stile and back lining each ⅞", the complete depth of the box can easily be determined. The width of the box is ascertained by: the thickness of the sash, which regulate the sash pockets (in the example shown on Plate 24 this dimension is 1½"); the width taken up by the parting strip (½"); and the width necessary for the stop bead which keeps the lower sash in place. This stop can be made as small as 1", but its usual width is 2" or more. The latter size gives better fastening space for cutains, shades, etc. The thickness of the stop is usually ½", thus making the face of the outside lining, the parting strip, and the window stop all on a line, each projecting as it does ½" beyond the face of the pulley stile.

(3)—The inside finish and mouldings are drawn, and the sash shown in the inside sash pocket. The dimension from the face of the pulley stile to the glass is usually 2", and the thickness of the moulding and the putty holding the glass in place is ⅜" or ½". The inside jamb casing is shown ⅞" thick and the veneer ¼". The window stop should cover the joint of the veneer; and the inside architrave or trim should cover the joint made by the jamb casing. In 9" brick walls the inside jamb casing and the veneer are usually omitted for lack of space; and the window stop and trim should overlap, or a small strip of veneer be inserted to cover the joint. In the best work a ground should be set to come flush with the face of plaster, to act as a level and provide for the secure nailing of the trim.

In the steps taken in drawing the section through the sill, it will be noticed that the detail of the plan of the window frame is so placed on the drawing that the members may easily be projected to the section detail of the sill. The same method of procedure is used as in drawing the plan detail, the width of the wall and the section through the masonry sill being drawn in first. The outside wood sill

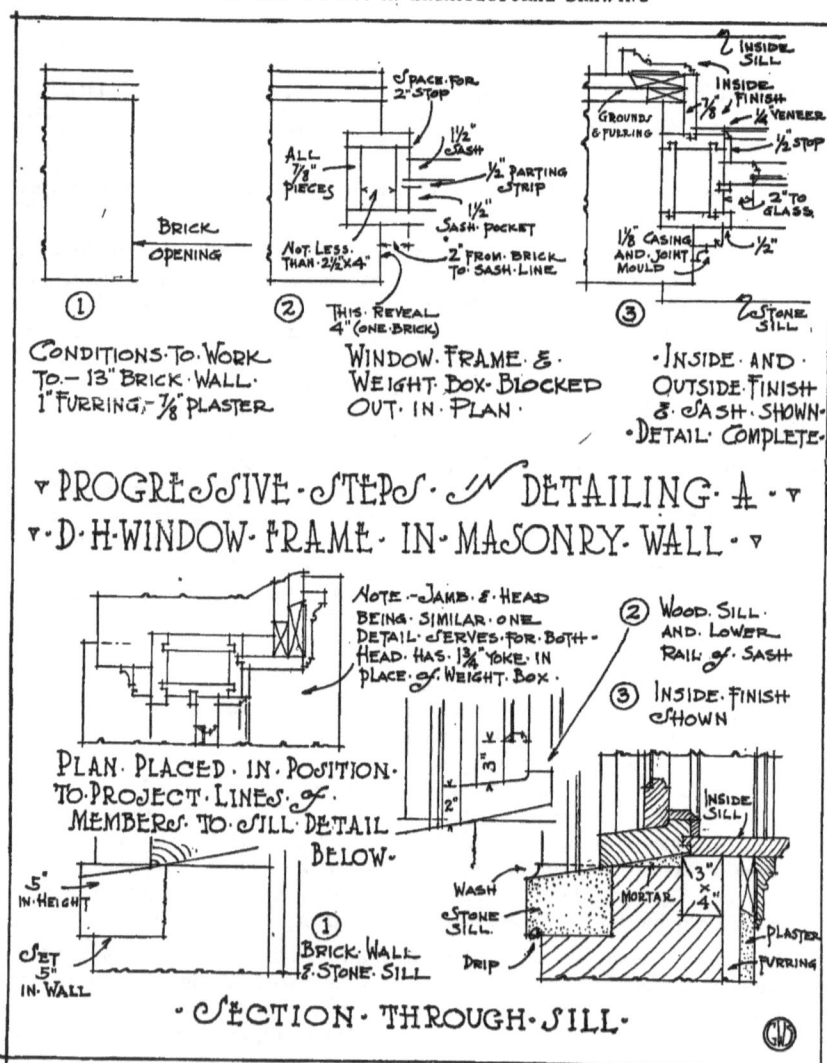

should be from 1¾" to 2¼" in thickness, and set on a pitch to make it more watertight. Sometimes the sill has the upper surface rabbeted to receive the screen. It will also be noticed that the lower surface is shown at a greater angle of pitch than the upper, thus securing a maximum thickness of the sill for the amount of material used. The back of the sill is rabbeted to receive the inside wood sill or stool. The sill is cut to a sharp wash where it meets the lower rail of the sash.

The window stop and veneer are shown to conform to the plan, and the inside sill, usually of 1⅛" material, projects with a moulded nosing far enough to cover the apron or trim below. The lower rail of the sash is usually shown 3"-wide from the sill to the glass. The projection of the masonry sill beyond the wall is about 1". Furring, plaster, and ground are in the same relation as shown on the plan.

Where a wide outside architrave is used in place of the 2" reveal of frame as here shown, the back lining of the box sets flush with the opening instead of being recessed. The frame should have a 2" x 3" piece nailed to sides and top to form a wind-break and anchor. The frame should also be set nearer the face of the wall, bringing the joint moulding forward so as to show about 1" of brickwork in the jambs. See illustration on Plate 23.

In stud walls omit the inside veneer and jamb casing, and have the outside architrave flush with the outside finish of the building. Also omit the back lining, as the stud forms the back of the weight box. For further study and reference consult Plates 22 and 23.

PROGRESSIVE STEPS IN THE DRAWING OF THREE-QUARTER AND FULL SIZE DETAILS

In the working out of a detail of any part of the building, the draughtsman must first ascertain the conditions or limitations to "work to." Indicate these correctly and then proceed with the drawing.

In the example, Plate 25, in drawing a detail of the main cornice, the wall plate is set above the attic floor joists to gain height in the attic. The height of the plate should always be determined in relation to the attic floor line as shown on ¼" scale elevations. Often for economy in construction, and to have a low cornice line in elevation, both the rafters and attic floor joists rest on the wall plate, as shown on Plate 17.

The steps taken in drawing the cornice detail may be described as follows:

(1)—Draw the top of the brick wall, either 9" or 13" thick.

(2)—Draw the plate and rafter foot, with the correct roof pitch, and locate the attic floor joists. The plate is usually 2" x 6", 2" x 8" or 3" x 8". The details above are determined by conditions as shown on the ¼" scale elevations of the house.

(3)—Indicate the lines of the sheathing and roof material each 1" thick, and drawn until they intersect the line marking the extreme projection of the cornice. This should be scaled from the ¼" scale elevations.

(4)—Draw the top and bottom lines of the finished cornice as scaled from the ¼" elevations, and then the profile and soffit in their correct positions.

(5)—The position of the sunk gutter should be determined and drawn, allowing enough space around it for blocking and supports. The gutter should not cut too deeply into the rafters. The main rafters may project to receive the cornice, or for economy, shorter length main rafters may be used ending at the face of the wall. If these latter are used short pieces or blocking must be spiked to the ends of these rafters and to the plate, for the support of the cornice.

(6)—The modillions and bed mould should be drawn to conform with the ¼" scale elevations. The nailing pieces for the cornice and bed mould are shown. Provision must be made for blocking to support the cornice. The tin lining of the gutter should project down over the edge, and up under the slate or shingles far enough to make the gutter water-tight. Anchor bolts are indicated. These should be approximately 4'-0" on centers, and should be placed in the wall as it is being built. All lettering and cross-hatching should be put in last. All finishing woodwork should be ⅞" thick, except mouldings which are heavier.

STEPS IN DRAWING DETAILS OF CORNICES

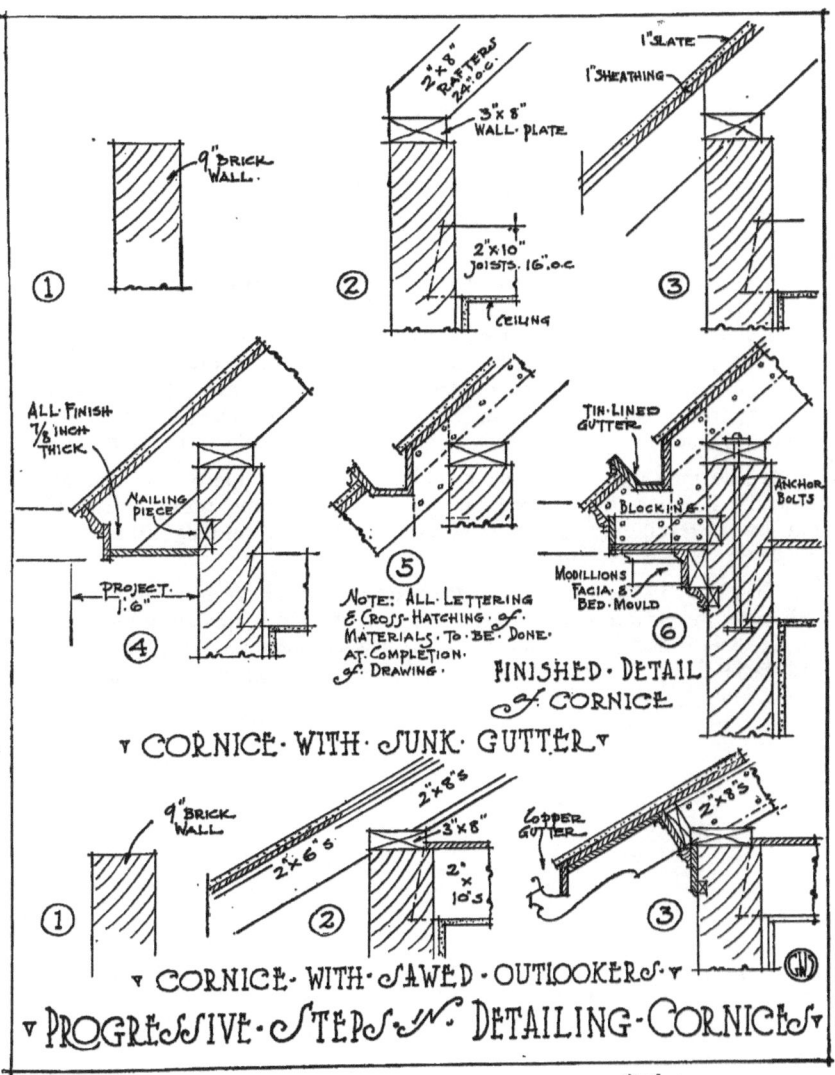

Plate 25

MOULDINGS AND PROFILES

A draughtsman should be familiar with the various mouldings and profiles most commonly used in architectural drawing, and be able to designate them by their technical names. He should practice continually on the drawing of profiles, both at ¼" scale and at full size, so that he will be able to draw them rapidly and correctly. He will find that even the most complicated cornice, belt-course, architrave, or trim is made up of simple curves, fillets, and facias, joined together in proper arrangement and proportion to obtain the desired effect when seen as a whole.

It is as important to have the mouldings in good proportion as it is to have the entire building proportioned correctly, and if the draughtsman understands the units he can readily draw an entire group of mouldings, forming either a cornice, architrave, belt-course, cap, or base.

On Plate 26 are shown some of the principal mouldings drawn to a large scale, and below them the profiles of some entire cornices at a smaller scale. By comparing these it may be seen how, with the various mouldings used in connection with facias or flat surfaces, almost any design of moulding or profile can be formed.

MOULDINGS AND PROFILES 49

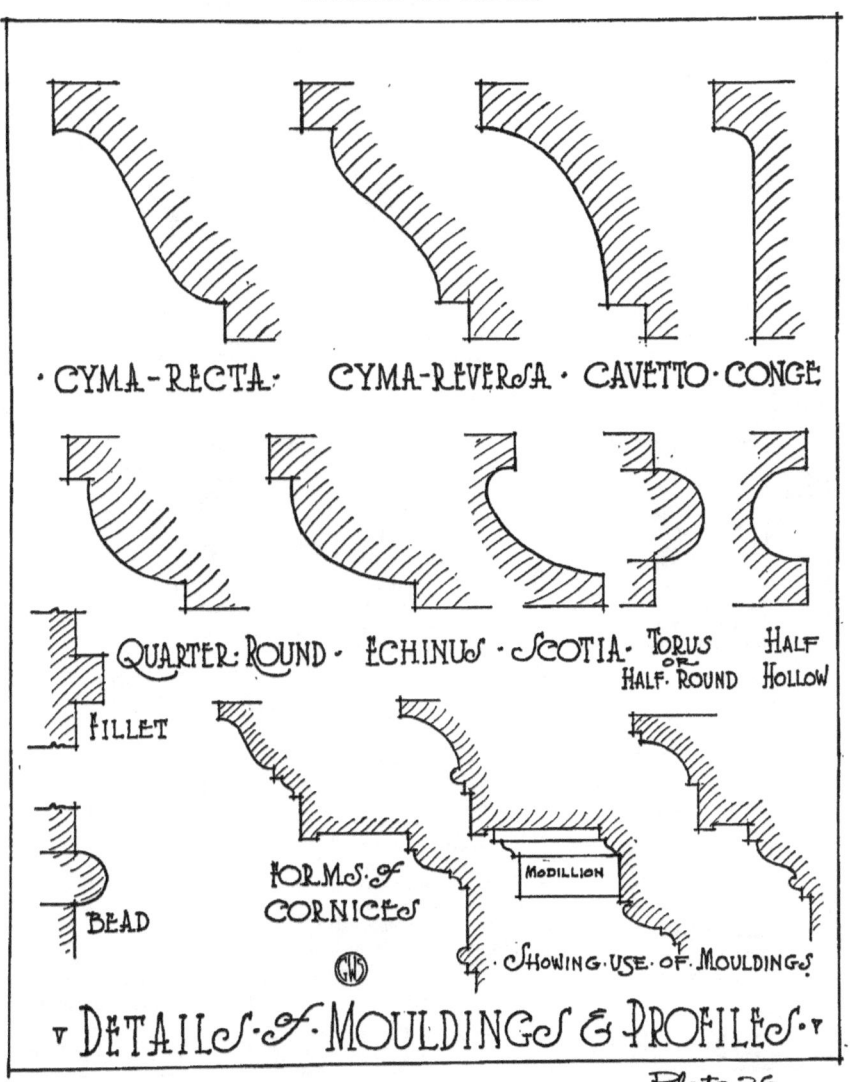

Plate 26

PROGRESSIVE STEPS IN ARCHITECTURAL DRAWING

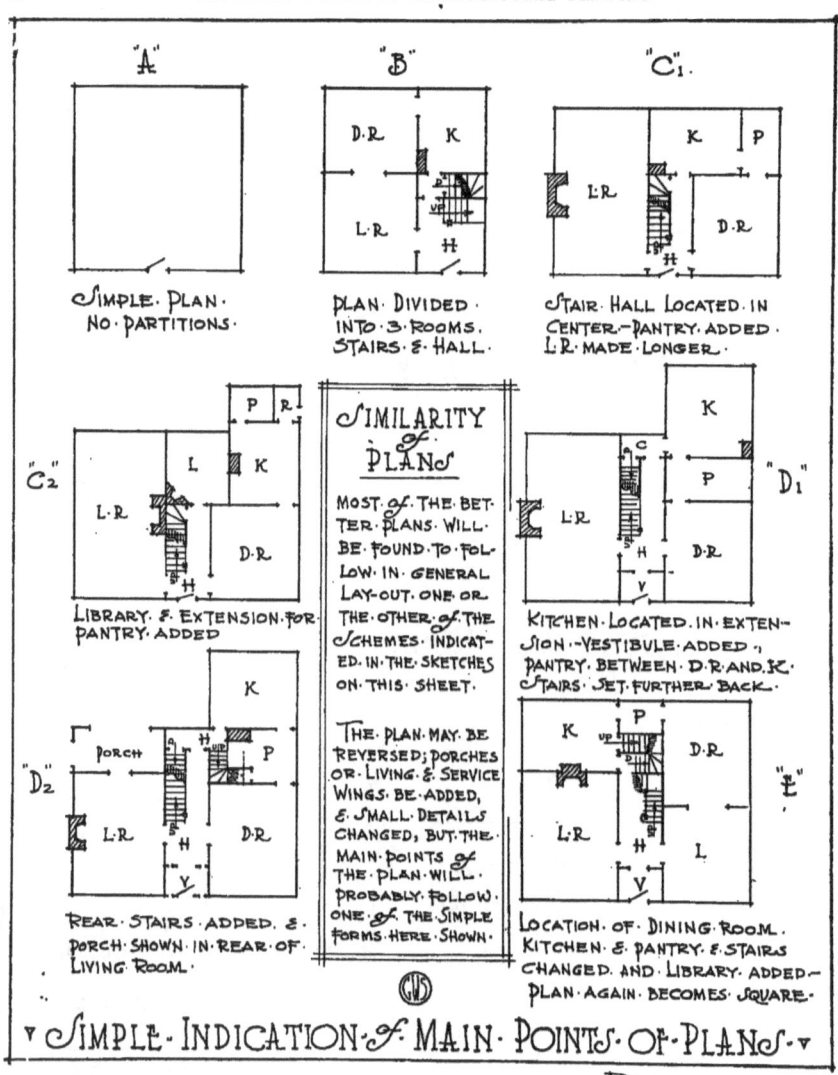

Plate 27

SINGLE LINE SKETCHES

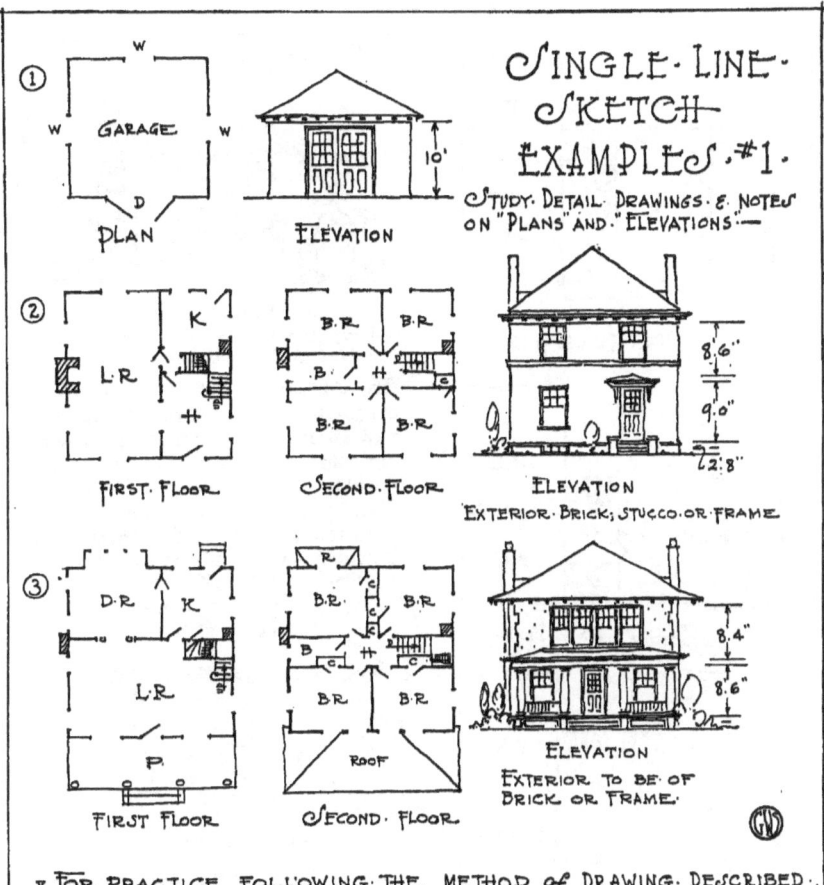

For practice following the method of drawing described on the preceding plates, single line sketches are here shown to be worked out by the student. For simplicity overall dimensions are given instead of sizes of rooms. — Garage 20'×20' inside. Houses 28'.0" wide × 32'.0" deep. — Exterior walls either brick or frame.

Plate 28

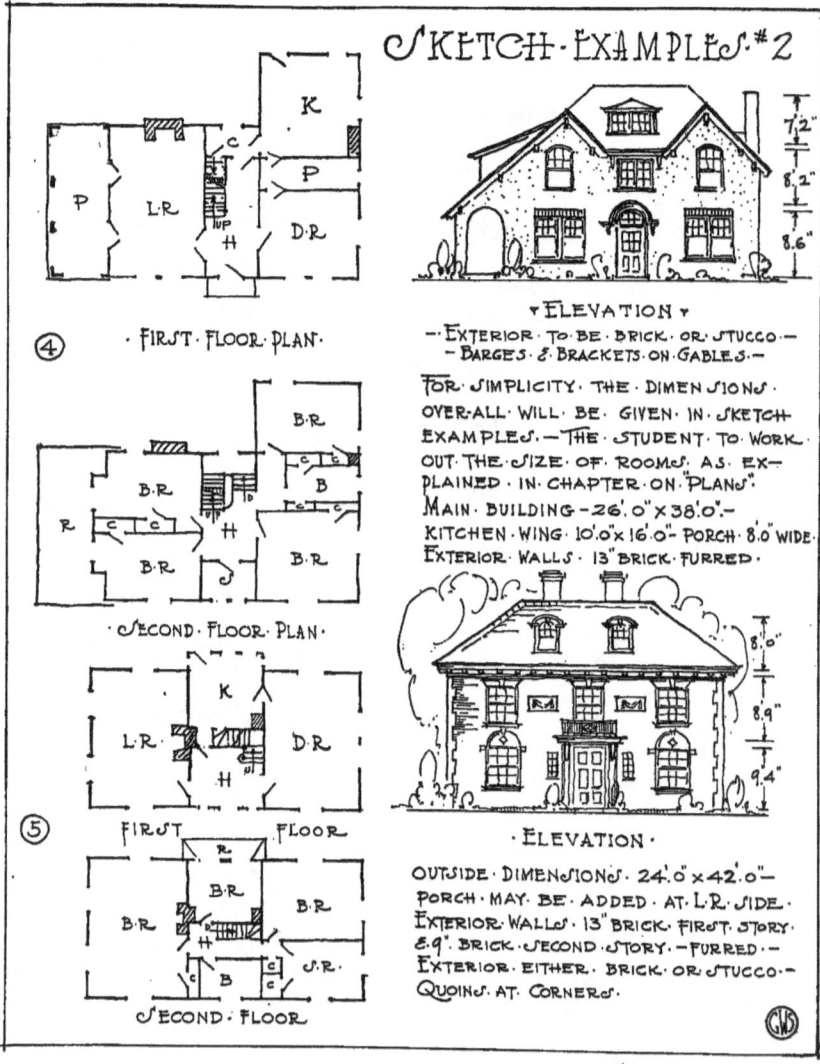

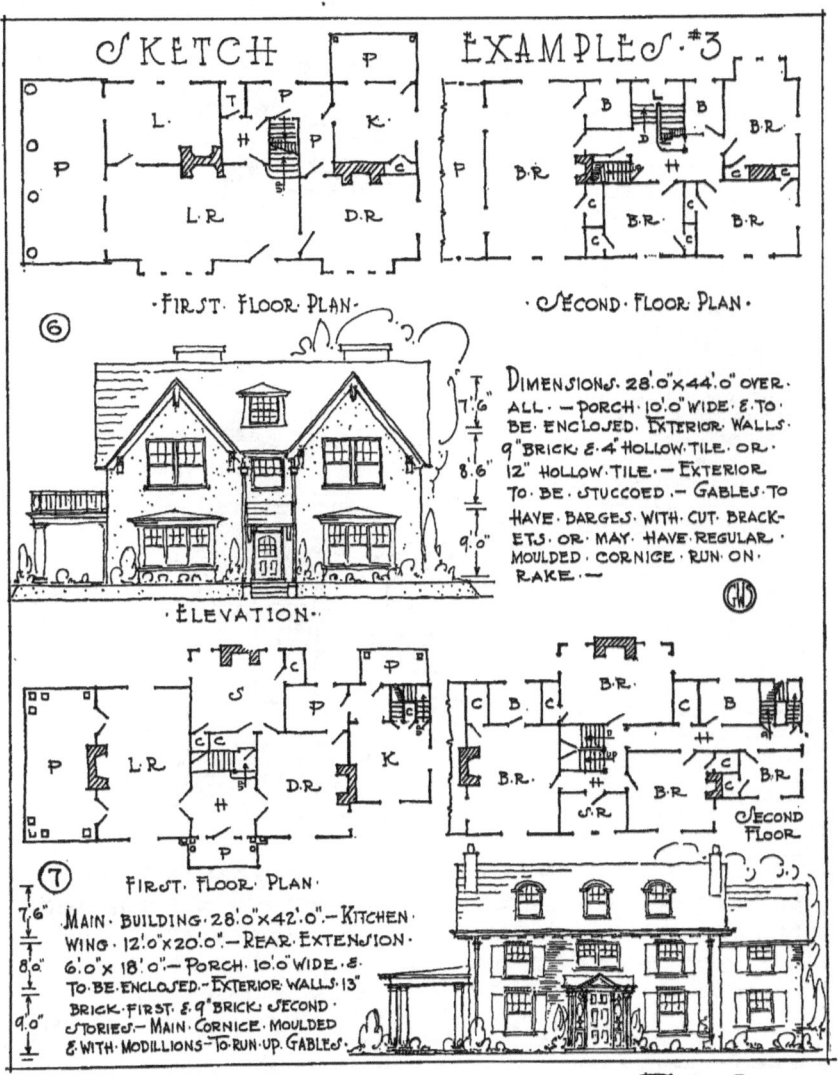

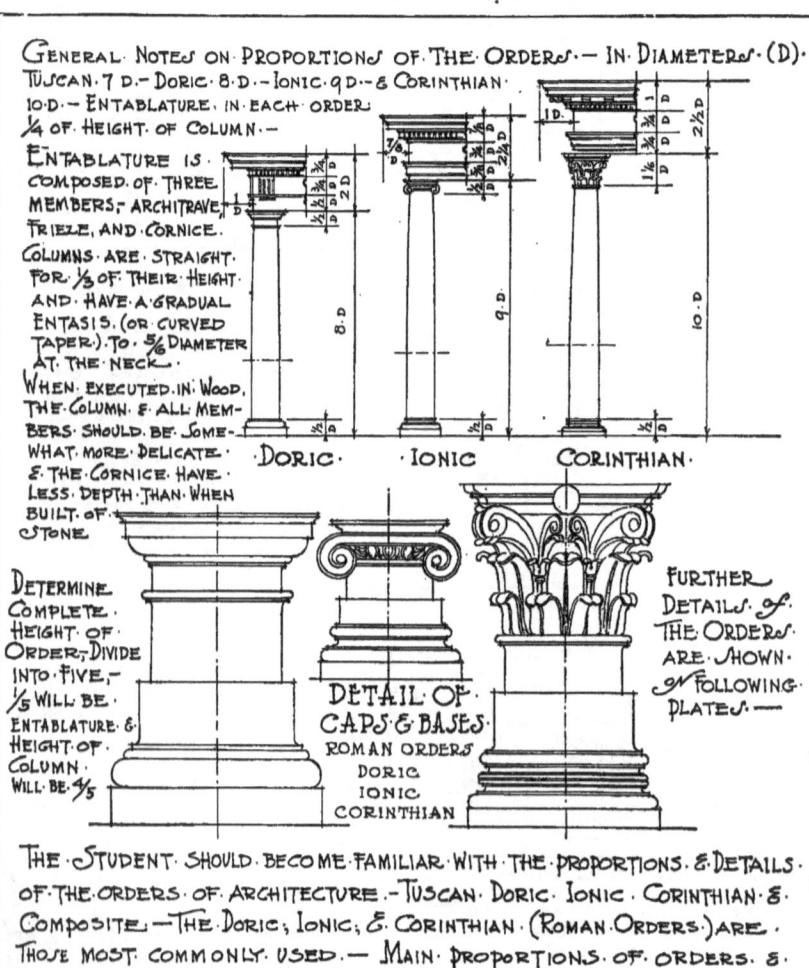

Plate 31

ORDERS OF ARCHITECTURE

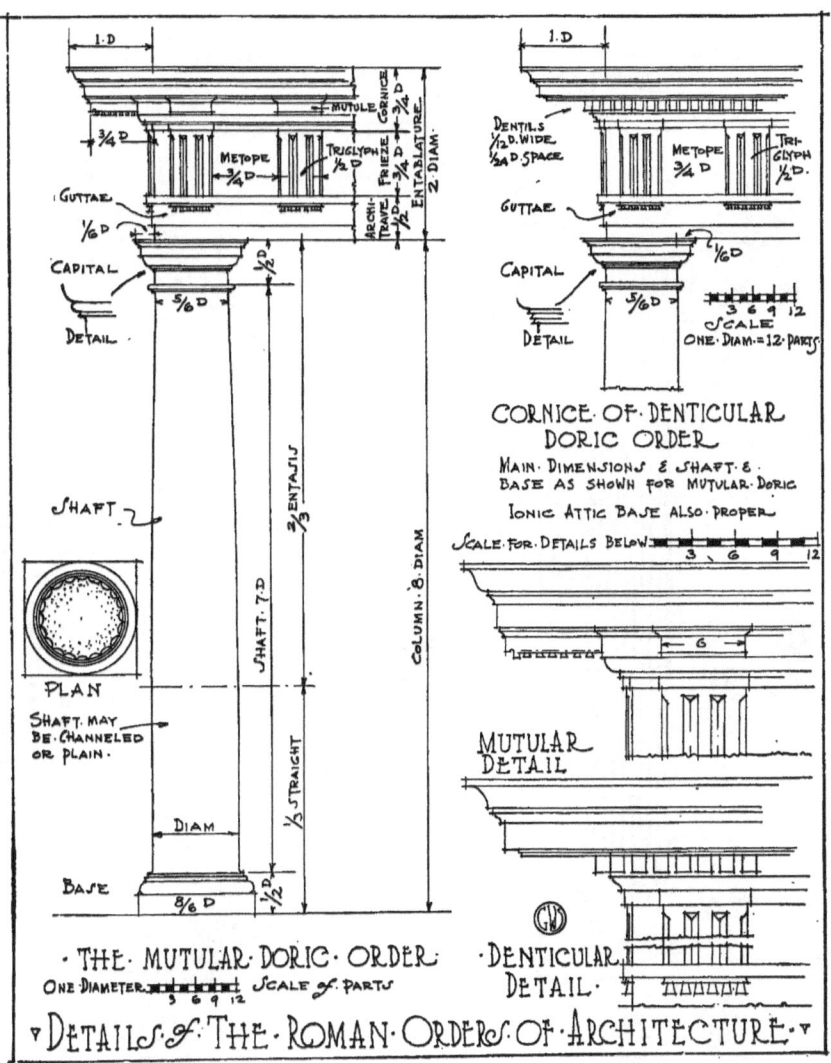

DETAILS OF THE ROMAN ORDERS OF ARCHITECTURE

Plate 32

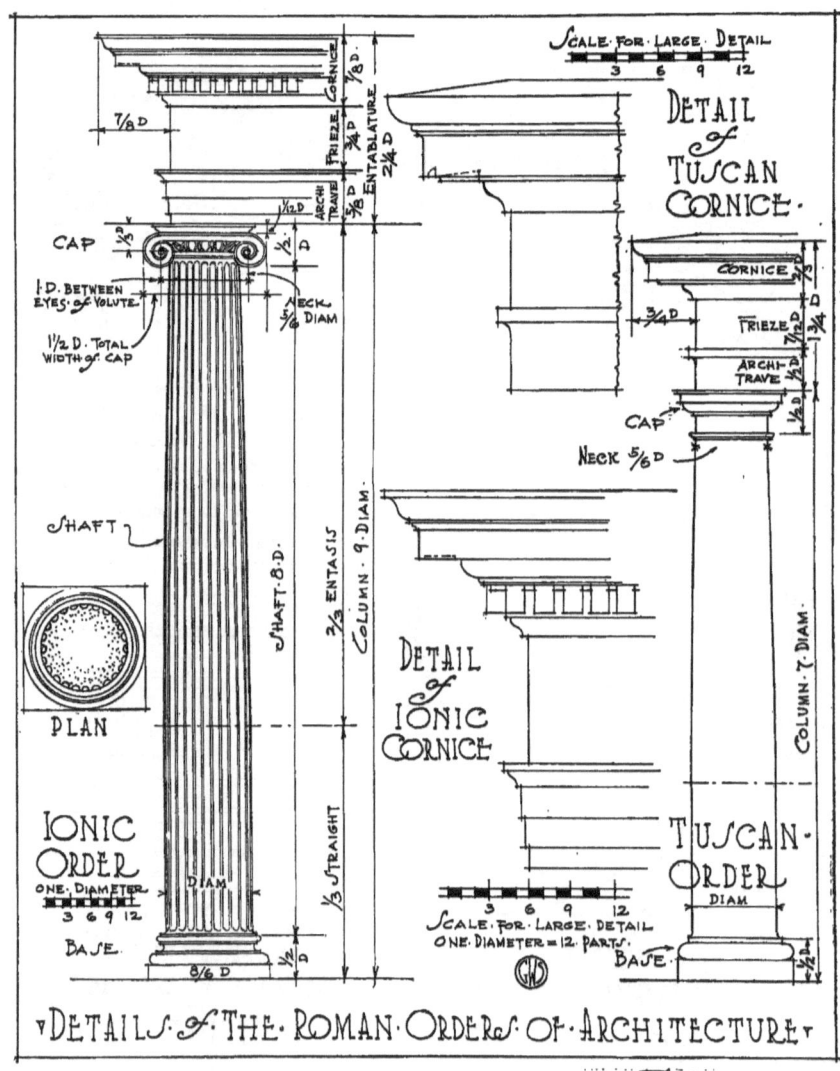

ORDERS OF ARCHITECTURE

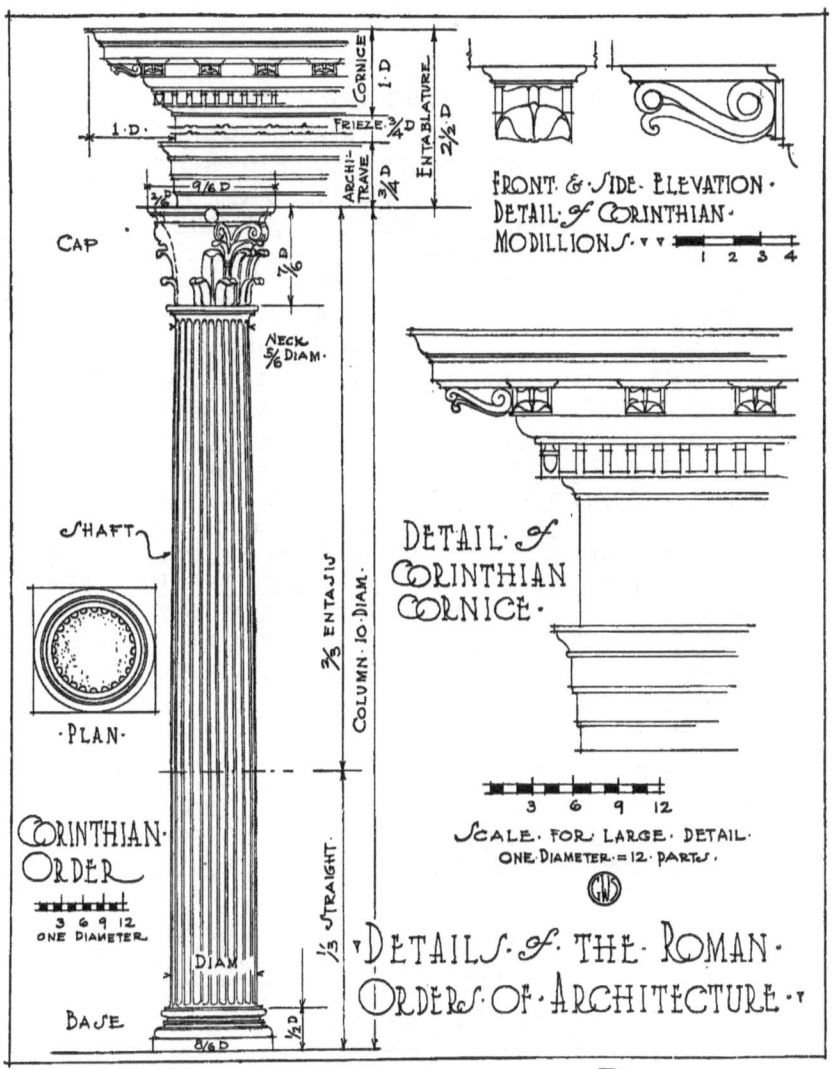

Plate 34

LETTERING · WHEN · WELL · DESIGNED · AND · PLACED · ADDS · GREATLY · TO · THE · INTEREST · & · PROFESSIONAL · APPEARANCE · OF · THE · DRAWING. ∞ AVOID · MECHANICAL · LETTERING · & · TECHNIQUE · IN ARCHITECTURAL · DRAWINGS; WHICH · SHOULD · DISPLAY · THE · INDIVIDUAL · TECHNIQUE · & · FREEDOM · of · THE · ARCHITECTURAL · DRAUGHTSMAN. ▾▾▾ EXCEPT · IN · SPECIAL · INSTANCES · ALL · LETTERING · SHOULD · BE · CAREFULLY · CONTAINED · BETWEEN · THE · GUIDE · LINES ∞ THOUGH · THE · CIRCULAR · LETTERS · C · G · O · Q · & · S · MAY · BE · SLIGHTLY · LARGER · ▾▾
∞ MOST · of · THE · LETTERS · EXCEPT · THESE · SHOULD · BE · NARROW · & · SNAPPY. ∽ THUS · A · B · D · E · F · H · J · K · L · M · N · P · R · T · U · V · W · X · Y · &c · THE · CIRCULAR · LETTERS · HOWEVER · SHOULD · BE · DRAWN · FULL · & · ROUND · THUS · C · G · O · Q · RATHER · THAN · C · G · O · Q ▾ THE · S · MAY · BE · NARROW · THE · PREPOSITIONS *of* · *in* *for* *from* & "*The*" · MAY · BE · USED · IN · SCRIPT · FORM · SPARINGLY · IF · BY · SO · DOING · THE · DESIGN · of · THE · LETTERING · IS · IMPROVED · ∞∞ OCCASIONALLY · ALSO · LETTERING · MAY · BE · OVERLAPPED · THUS · – NORTH – CORINTH – FLOOR · ETC · ▾ THE · TAILS · of · THE · R · & · THE · J · MAY · ALSO · EXTEND · BELOW · THE · LINE · BUT · NOT · TOO · FREQUENTLY. – FORMS · SUCH · AS · ▾ ∞ ▵ WHEN · USED · CORRECTLY · & · SPARINGLY · ADD · TO · THE · DESIGN · & · BALANCE · of · THE · LETTERING · ▾▾▾ ·

▾ THE · CROSSING · OF · LINES · IN · ARCHITECTURAL · DRAWING · SHOULD · NOT · BE · THOUGHT · BY · THE · BEGINNER · TO · INDICATE · HASTE · OR · CARELESSNESS · BUT · IS · A · STUDIED · EFFORT · ON · THE · PART · of · THE · DRAUGHTSMAN · TO · PRODUCE · A · CRISP; SNAPPY · DRAWING · THUS ·

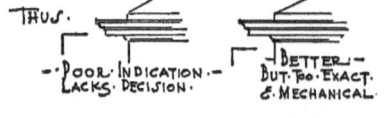

– POOR · INDICATION · – LACKS · DECISION ·

– BETTER – BUT · TOO · EXACT · & MECHANICAL ·

– CORRECT · DRAWING · – LINES · SLIGHTLY · INTERSECTING · – GIVING · SNAP · TO · THE · DRAWING · – SHOULD · BE · CAREFULLY · DONE · SO · AS · NOT · TO · CONFUSE · PROFILES ·

▾ HINTS · ON · LETTERING ▾ TECHNIQUE ▾ ETC · ▾

Plate 35

▼ARCHITECTURAL · LETTERING ᵉfor.
Use ᴺ The · Preparation · of ·
Competitive · &ᶜ Working · · ▼
Drawings · ▼

· Alphabet · ▼ ABCDEFGHIJKL ·
MNOPQRSTUVWXYZ · &ᶜ ▼
1234567890 · &ᶜ Small · ABCDEFGHI
JKLMNOPQRSTUVWXYZ ·

Also · script · alphabet ▼ abcdefghijk
lmnopqrstuv wxyz · &c · 1234567890 · ▼
Used · for · notes · and · fast · work · ▼

· *OBLIQUE · 1234567890* ▼ *ABC
DEFGHIJKLMNOPQRSTUVW-
XYZ · &ᶜ · Small · script · alphabet · abc
defghijklmnopqrstuvwxyz · &c.* ▼▼▼

▼ Front · Elevation ▼ East · West · North ·
▼ South · ▼ First · Floor · Plan · Second · ▼
▼ Foundation · Attic · Side · & · Rear · ▼▼
▼ A · Page · ᴺ Lettering · ▼

Plate 36

INDEX

(NUMBERS REFER TO PAGES)

A

Anchor Bolt	46, 47
Arches, Flat Stone	35, 36
Architrave, Inside	43, 44
Of Entablature	54, 55, 56, 57
Outside	12, 41
Areas, Window	12
Arrow Heads	21
Ash Dump	22

B

Band, Projecting Brick	24, 28
Barge	33, 52, 53
Base, Column	40, 54, 55, 56, 57
Detail	42
Outlet	22
Bathroom	11
Bathtub	12, 22
Bed Mould	29, 33, 34, 39, 47
Bedroom	11
Blinds	37
Blocking	34, 46, 47
Boiler	12, 20, 22
Bracket	13, 33, 36, 37
Brick	14, 20, 22, 30

C

Capital	54, 55, 56, 57
Casing	36, 42, 43, 44
Cellar	12
Center Lines	10, 14, 15, 19, 24
Chimney	14, 25, 27
Brick Cap	33
Cut Stone Cap	33
Elevations	33
Flues	11, 14, 22
Height	32
Rough Cast	33
Terra Cotta Top	33
Closet	12, 22
Cold Closet	32

Column, Chamfered	37
Channeled	37, 55, 56, 57
Details	39, 54, 55, 56, 57
Paneled	37
Porch	12, 37, 39
Round	37
Square	37
Conductor Heads	37
Cornice, Blocked Out	24, 26
Box	34
Details	34, 39, 46, 47, 49
Elevations	33
Gable	33
Of Entablature	54, 55, 56, 57
Overhanging	33
Plain	33
Profiles	29, 31
Cross-hatching	14, 20, 22

D

Dentil	55
Details, Arch	35
Columns	39
Cornices	34, 46, 47, 49
Exterior	12, 22, 37
Fixtures	22
Interior	11, 22
Modillions	34
Outlookers	34, 46, 47
Segment Heads	35
Windows	35, 36, 41, 42, 44
Dining-room	11, 19
Door, Closet	11
Double	11
Frame	22, 41
Head	29
Openings	11, 13, 14, 18, 22, 27
Outside	11, 20, 22, 32
Size	13
Dormers	30, 31
Flat Roof	36

INDEX

Gable Head	36
Hip Roof	36
Segment Head	36
Sill Lines	31, 36
Drawing	10
Cross-hatching	14, 20, 22
Hints	10
Inking	21, 41
Lettering	20, 21, 58, 59
Lines	10, 14, 15, 19, 20, 21
Notes	30, 31
Sketches	7, 8, 51, 52, 53
System of Lay-out	7, 10
Ticking Off	24
Dresser	12, 20, 22

E

Electric Outlets	14, 20, 22
Switches	14
Elevations	12, 24, 30
Chimneys	33
Cornices	33, 37
Dormers	36
Gables	33
Porches	37
Sketches	8, 51, 52, 53
Entablature	40, 54, 55, 56, 57
Entasis	40, 54, 55, 56, 57
Entrance, Front	30, 32

F

Facia	38, 34, 47
Fireplace	14, 20, 22, 32
First Story	12
Fixtures	12, 22
Floor Line	12
Frieze	40, 54, 55, 56, 57
Furring	41, 42, 44

G

Gable	33
Head Dormer	36
Gas Outlet	14
Glass Sizes	12, 30
Grade Line	12, 24, 37
Gusset Board	28, 31

Guttae	55
Gutter, Box	33, 34, 37, 39
Hanging	33, 37
Moulded	33
Sunk	33, 34, 47

H

Hall	11, 19
Head, Door	24, 28
Window	24, 28
Hollow Tile	14, 20, 22
Hood, Door	36, 37

I

Inking, Entasis of Column	40
Rules for	9, 21, 58

J

Joint Mould	41, 43, 44
Joists	34, 47
Attic Floor	47

K

Kitchen	11, 12, 19
Keystones	13, 28, 35, 36, 37

L

Landing, Stair	23
Laundry Tub	22
Lavatory	12, 22
Lettering	20, 21, 58, 59
Lines, Center	10, 14, 15, 19
Cross-hatch	20
Dimension	20
Inking of	21, 58
Intersection of	9, 21, 58
Over-all Dimension	20, 21
Projection	20
Living-room	11, 19

M

Materials, Indication of	20, 22, 30
Metope	55
Modillion	29, 33, 38, 39, 47, 57
Moulding, Bead	49

Bed	29, 31, 39	Plate	34, 46, 47
Cap	36	Porch	20
Cavetto	49	Baluster	37
Conge	49	Columns	37
Cyma-Recta	49	Floor	13, 37
Cyma-Reversa	49	Heights	13
Details	48, 49	Lattice	37
Echinus	49	Location	32
Half-Hollow	49	Rail	13, 37
Joint	41	Steps	14
Lines	29, 31, 39	Profile	38, 39, 49
Quarter-Round	49	Pulley Stile	43, 44
Scotia	49	Purlin	33
Torus	49		
Muntin	30, 31, 35, 36		
Mutule	55		

N

Newel 23
Notes, Location on Drawing........... 30, 31

O

Opening, Dimensioning 20, 21
  Door 20, 22, 27
  Window 12, 13, 22, 27
Orders of Architecture........... 54, 55, 56, 57
  Corinthian 54, 57
  Doric 54, 55
  Ionic 54, 56
Outlooker 33, 37
  Details 34, 46, 47

P

Pantry 11, 19
  Window Openings 12
Parting Strip 43, 44
Partitions 14, 17
Pencils 10
Piers 12, 20, 37
Pilaster 37
Plans 10, 14, 20
  Details 22, 23
  Similarity 50
  Sketch 8, 51, 52, 53
  Variations 50

Q

Quoin, Brick or Stone.............. 33, 52

R

Radiator 14, 20, 22
Rafter 12, 34
  Ends 33
  Foot 46, 47
  Main 46, 47
  Show 13
Rail, Lower Sash.................. 44, 45
  Meeting 44
Range 12, 20, 22
Reveal, Frame 41, 43, 44
Rise of Stair........................ 23
Roof, Blocked Out................. 24, 26
  Pitch 13, 24
  Ridge Line 24, 25
  Shingle 13
  Slag 13
  Slate 13, 36
  Tin 13, 36
Room, Bath 11
  Bed 11
  Dining 11, 20
  Living 11, 20
  Location 10, 20
  Shape 11, 20
  Size 10, 11, 20
  Sketches 50, 51, 52, 53

INDEX

S

Sash	35, 36, 44, 45
Pockets	42, 43, 44
Second Story	12
Shaft	54, 55, 56, 57
Sheathing	34, 41, 46, 47
Shingles	13, 46, 47
Slate	13, 36, 47
Wood	13
Shutter	43, 44
Sink, Kitchen	12, 20, 22
Sill, Brick	13, 35
Details	41, 42, 44
Door	13
Heights	24
Inside	41, 42, 43, 44
Outside	41, 42, 43, 44
Stone	13, 35, 41, 42
Window	11, 12, 41
Wood	13, 35, 36, 42, 45
Sketches, Architect's	7, 8, 51, 52, 53
Skew Block	13, 35
Soffit	33
Soil Pipe	12
Stairs	14, 19, 23
Head Room	23
Landing	23
Main	23
Method of Figuring	23
Rear	23
Riser	23
Tread	23
Stone	22, 30
Stool	44, 45
Stop Bead	43, 44
Details	42
Window	43, 44
Story Heights	24, 25, 51, 53
Stucco	52, 53

T

"Ticking"	24, 40
Tile, Hearth	22
Tin Roof	36, 37
Title	20, 21
Transom	35
Tread	23
Trim, Door	41, 42
Inside	41, 42, 43, 44
Window	41, 42, 44
Tryglyph	55

V

Variations in Plans	32
Veneer	42, 43, 44
Vestibule	19
Volute	54, 56

W

Walls	11, 14, 20
Brick	13
Hollow Tile	14
Stud	22
Wash Tray	12
Water Table	13, 24, 35
Weight Box	41, 42, 43, 44
Wind Break	42, 45
Window	11, 20
Architrave	41, 44
Casement	11, 22, 35
Cellar	22, 41
Details	41, 42, 43, 44
Dormer	30, 31, 36
Double Hung	22, 35, 41, 42, 43, 44
Finish	41, 42, 43, 44
Frame	35, 36
French	22
Heads	13, 35, 41
Jamb	41, 42, 44
Opening	12, 13, 27
Panes	12
Sill Heights	11, 12
Sills	11, 13, 35, 41, 44, 45

www.ingramcontent.com/pod-product-compliance
Lightning Source LLC
Chambersburg PA
CBHW052215240426
43670CB00037B/637